THE HUNTED &
THE HUNTER

W9-BWH-244

THE HUNTED &
THE HUNTER

The Search for the Secret Tomb of
CHINGGIS QA'AN

Alan Nichols

REGENT PRESS
Berkeley, California

Copyright © 2017 Alan Nichols

[hardback]
ISBN 13: 978-1-58790-427-1
ISBN 10: 1-58790-427-6

[paperback]
ISBN 13: 978-1-58790-419-6
ISBN 10: 1-58790-419-5

[e-book]
ISBN 13: 978-1-58790-420-2
ISBN 10: 1-58790-420-9

Library of Congress Control Number: 2017953131

The pictures in this book are mostly original.
Where they are sourced from public and private venues
we have attempted to find and request permission.

The unattributed quotations in bold italics in the beginning
of each chapter are from the author's compendium
"ALANQUOTES"

Manufactured in the U.S.A.
REGENT PRESS
Berkeley, California
www.regentpress.net

Table of Contents

EXPLORATION POSTSCRIPTS

In The Beginning ...
The Hunted & The Hunter

"It's harder to find why you are searching than to find what you're looking for."

Alan Nichols, the hunter, on the Khenzimane Pass near Lhasa, Tibet in 2007.

The statue of Chinggis Qa'an, the hunted, in the northern Mongolian area where he was born and raised.

According to the *Secret History of the Mongols:* "**At the beginning there was blue-grey wolf, born with destiny ordained by Heaven Above**". And from his union with the fallow doe on Sacred Mount Burkhan Khaldun came the lineage of the greatest warrior and largest empire in the history of our world.

Named Temujin as a boy born in 1161, he fights his way to veneration in 1206 as Chinggis Qa'an (erroneously aka Genghis Khan), meaning a strong, wolf-like leader of leaders. (Nicknamed "CQ" in our account.)

The Hunter in our story, a decorated officer in the Korean War, is born in 1930, named after his uncle honored in World War I by France with the Croix de Guerre for his heroism as a fighter pilot. The Hunter is the leader of the expedition to find the tomb of CQ and also undertakes the nine years of research about the last days of CQ to find the secret tomb of the Hunted.

This book includes two histories of the search for the tomb of CQ. CQ's story is based on the knowledge we have of him, slight, inaccurate and biased as it may be. There are two sides to every story in this book — the life of CQ and the Hunter's stories of the search for his secret tomb.

The pictures are mostly from the last expedition and the internet. The findings are original and unprecedented. They all relate to the exploration and study of the death and burial of CQ, his last 30 days, his secret funeral cortege, his burial site on Mountain X.

The overall story of the *The Hunted and the Hunter* can be found here in the public reports from the *South China Mountain Post*

(SCMP), and on the lighter side some fake news about the discovery.

This newly-told saga will transform the reader's ideas about exploration, CQ, field expeditions, the Mongol empire, and historical psychology.

The book includes the summary results of years of research in the first published recitation of the specific qualifications that must be met to find CQ's gravesite. These findings are again confirmed in this expedition. But on this journey we encounter the potentially disastrous unconscious development of a tourist complex unknowingly built on CQ's grave. And we explore the site with extraordinarily singular modern technology employed clandestinely.

The secrecy, history and sacredness of Mountain X is an epic in itself.

We know relatively little about CQ and the Mongol empire taking into account their historical importance, but we do know his tomb will be a revelation of exceptional knowledge about CQ's personality and his empire and culture.

For the first time in modern published analysis we reveal the psycho-history of the world's greatest conqueror along with the psychological comparison of CQ with the Hunter, both studies in hubris, perseverance, and deception.

And in this story we solve a major historical mystery as to how his family and his army were able to secretly bury and move the corpse hundreds of miles from his deathbed to his gravesite.

Our epic ends with an enlightenment of the Hunter in the newly built Tibetan temple on Mountain X and the true basis of our success.

For his times CQ, energetic and very active, dies an old man at 67. Alan, the Hunter, the author and Leader, is still alive, energetic and vital at 87, also an old man for his times.

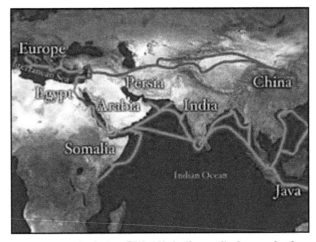

Alan cycled the Silk Web (in red) through the Middle East conquered by Chinggis and his family and traveled by Marco Polo (red and blue) on behalf of CQ's grandson and founder of the Yuan Dynasty, Kublai Qa'an.

Grandson Max carrying the Hunter (Alan) across the Onon, CQ's home territory in Mongolia.

1.
How To Find the Tomb of Chinggis Qa'an

*"Research is the first road, the high road,
the indispensable way, to find
the grave of CQ."*

**A Chinese version of CQ. We don't know what
CQ really looks like but surely not like this.**

GRAVE TRUTHS

Many have tried (starting famously with Marco Polo) to find the Tomb of Chinggis Qa'an (CQ). All have failed until now. Our expedition spends nine years tracking the possibilities, the histories, the sources, and our instincts to set the criteria for locating the gravesite.

Mountain X is the only place that satisfies all these requirements:

Secrecy

CQ and his family, along with their Shaman advisers, are determined to keep his burial place secret. They accomplish this for over 750 years. They do all they can to avoid discovery. To find the Tomb any search must take that into account.

Shamanism

CQ is a follower of Mongolian shamanism and is daily governed by its advice and support. Therefore his burial place must conform to the following Mongol shaman criteria:

1. CQ must be buried in a place and in a casket consistent with shamanistic funeral practices.

Karakorum staging ground for CQ's armies, and built into an extraordinary capitol by his son and successor Ogedei, 1186-1241.

National Geographic

An expedition in Northern Mongolia using drones to find CQ's corpse.

According to tradition and legend CQs corpse was put in a silver casket. We doubt it. It's the wrong one.

2. Because of the evil forces that invade corpses ("the contagion of death"), CQ's corpse must be promptly buried, consisent with all shamanistic reqirements. (Some claim within fourteen days of death).

3. CQ must be buried strategically as may be necessary to carry out his afterlife missions: to protect his Mongolian people and to "bring the whole world under his sword," including particularly Southern China, the "Sung Empire."

Deception

The Qa'an and his successors are masters of deception in military tactics. The actual tomb location is hidden so that anyone looking for the burial place is intentionally deceived as to its location. The burial place therefore must reflect significant deceptions.

Sacred Mountain

CQ must be buried on a 13th century Sacred Mountain in ancient Mongolia.

Prior Searches

CQ obviously is not buried in a place that has already been extensively searched, especially with modern equipment. For example: Karakoram, the Ordos, Burkhan Khaldun in northern Mongolia and western Altai Mountains.

Legends

There should be at least oral or written legendary support for the actual location of the tomb site.

Intuition

Intuitive recognition as well as facts, histories and logic must be invoked in locating the tomb. Many important discoveries, including finding Mountain X, rely on instinct.

Cortege

The route from CQ's deathbed in the Liu Pan Mountains of China to his burial grounds in ancient Mongolia must allow for prompt, feasible and practical cart transport.

How can we miss finding the Tomb now! Will we, the Hunters, survive the legendary hex on anyone disturbing the Tomb of Chinggis Qa'an?

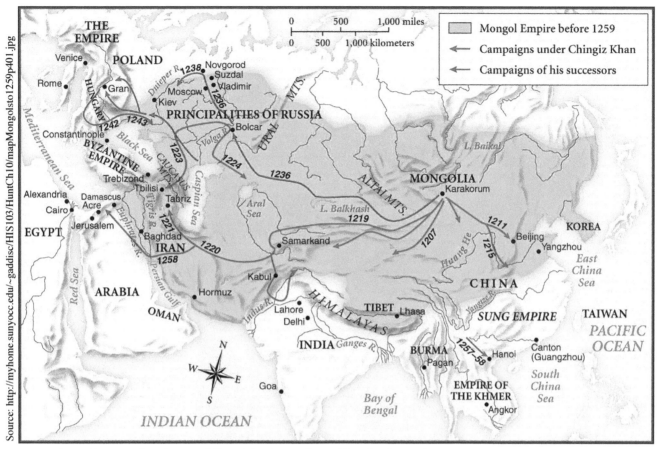

Source: http://myhome.sunyocc.edu/~gaddisc/HIS103/HuntCh10/mapMongolsto1259p401.jpg

The Mongol Empire as CQ left it. Note Sung Empire in white conquered by CQ's son and grandson as CQ directed on his deathbed. — important clue to finding CQs grave site.

Replica of the oxen pulling the cortege cart carrying CQ's corpse from the Liu Pan death site to the Mountain X gravesite. (Excellent mausoleum statues but the cart was actually pulled by camels.)

11

2.
The Bottom Line... 2016 Chinggis Qa'an (CQ) Tomb Expedition ... Thus Saith Mountain X

"In Life and worship the only way to understanding is to observe from all sides."

The only way to find out what Chinggis Qa'an really looks like is from his tomb.

Three years, thousands of hours of planning, research and organization by our Field Team, our Core team, our Advisory Team and True.lnk, and the huge expense of the 2016 Expedition to discover the secret grave of CQ, is made possible by our sponsors, especially Frederik Paulsen and his Mamont Foundation, the Sacred Mountain Foundation and *True* magazine.

We have been to Mountain X and the grave-site three times before. So, what more is there to do ...

1. Confirm the 10 criteria for locating the tomb. We accomplish that "in spades" in this expedition.

2. We establish the route of CQ's funeral cortege from the Liu Pan mountains, in Ningxia where CQ dies, to Mountain X, his burial site, to satisfy that tenth criteria and prove the feasibility and timeliness of taking CQ's casket from his death site to his burial site.

3. We confirm that Mountain X is part of ancient Mongolia and is truly a Sacred Mountain, both criteria for locating the grave of CQ.

Dr. Frederik Paulsen, famous polar explorer and Expedition Core Team Member.

4. We undertake a circumambulation over the rugged landscape of the Sacred Mountain, probably the first, which reconfirms its holy importance.

5. The expedition gathers a huge volume of magnetometry and ground penetrating radar (GPR) data for analysis. The best way to confirm our hypothesis would be to dig some test holes, but that is not allowed. We must prove with our technical data that CQ is buried here before we can excavate to prove what we already know.

Our proof must be extensive enough to "convince your grandmother" when we announce our results. That is *the bottom line.*

Mountain X is rugged country

Tracking our circumambulation.

Hiking The Middle Ridge . . . Mountain X. Alan and Stew circumambulating the mountain.

Vales and ridges around Mountain X.

Author climbing Sacred Mountain X.

3.
The Transitory Grave-Site

*"All things are transitory. The two rules
of life are change & death."*

**This is a movie version of Chinggis
Qa'an with the usual vicious
western touch.**

If only Mountain X, Chinggis Qa'an's boneyard, could talk, it could tell us it's multi-millennial history — geological, human, paleological, archeological, political and spiritual. The ultimate single word description for this Sacred Mountain is *"transitory"* — the constant transformation of existence.

Mountain X witnesses the rise of Chinese civilization along the Yellow River, the Mongol homelands, the multiple invasions and occupation by Chinggis Qa'an and his warriors on their way to conquer north China, and their invasion route for the first attack against the Tanguts and their Xia Xia empire to the south of Mongolia.

Chinggis Qa'an is always quick to change and adopt the military weaponry (siege machinery, explosives, logistics) and tactics of his enemies. He is said to have remarked, "I never fought the same battle twice."

The Mountain is a holy center since before recorded history. We know that sacredness is recognized by a Buddhist monastery for at least 400 years. And the monastery wouldn't have been built here but for the mountain's spiritual importance at that time.

Chinggis Qa'an and his Mongol Shaman recognize Mountain X as important spiritually when they are in the region with the army. Even today we can't miss its distinct

Behind the clouds of history lies the secret Tomb of Chinggis Qa'an.

position and shape.

In modern times as well as the 13th century, the area is a center of commerce and military conflict. When I first see the area surrounding Mountain X, it overlooks a changing modern industrialization amidst the historic grasslands and farmlands of ancient Mongolia. Border villages in nearby China are now population centers with extensive production and resource developments.

From my first discovery of the mountain in 2007 while on a diversion from my biking

the silk web (aka silk road) expedition and subsequent expeditions including my last visit in 2016, I see the change with highways, housing, factories, hotels, and commercial operations. The government's population transfer policy eliminates Mongols in favor of Han Chinese on the China side of the border.

The site we identify as Chinggis Qa'an's Tomb is now developed with a huge tourist infrastructure of temples, roads, and administration and tourist facilities. What that does to our expedition is another story we

A 400-year-old monastery. Its legendary history confirms the sacredness of Mountain X .

Border Villiage . . . Now an Urbanapolis in inner Mongolia.

will tell later.

Since my first ascent many years ago, the summit trail up Mountain X is improved. A tram lift to take tourists to the top is now being installed.

But underneath Mountain X lie the remains of a monastery and more significantly the grave of Chinggis Qa'an, deteriorating for 790 years but still containing invaluable artifacts.

Mountain X isn't what it used to be ... on the surface.

New construction on Mountain X.

4.
Oops...Mountain X Buried in Tourism

"There are no important victories without risks of defeat."

This is an imaginative middle ages European version of Chinggis Qa'an.

Before going overseas, our google earth searches of Mountain X reveal an astounding development. The whole Mountain X burial site is covered in buildings constructed since our last expedition in the fall of 2012. Then the site has no improvements other than the remains of a temple lamasery burned down in the Cultural Revolution in the 1960's by a local gang, consistent with the cultural genocide in China during that time, and a small garage size Han Buddhist temple at the bottom of the mountain.

The 400-year-old lamasery once housed a famous general and an important member of the royal family.

I panic. The new construction will make it impossible to use our equipment assum-

ing the buildings are locked. The new project can make investigating impossible because of interference with our underground testing equipment. In fact, ferrous underground rebar would scatter magnetic energies making magnetometry useless and our radar could also be blocked.

If we are unable to technologically search underground, the expedition might as well be cancelled. All these years of effort and dreaming seem wasted.

But we aren't ready to give up. Our team with research and talking to vendors find out we can test underground laterally with our equipment from surrounding open areas, outside patios and roads near the buildings. That still leaves a serious question as

Oops ... Some new site buildings.

to who is occupying this development: the Army, police, secret educational or government activities? A developer? And will they let us test, or fine us for working without a permit, or even throw us in jail?

At that point another hero of our Field Team, Yang Fan, who lives in Beijing, steps forward. He volunteers on a weekend to fly and drive to Mountain X to seek answers to our questions as to the feasibility, technically and politically, of gathering data with our magnetometry and GPR with unidentified strangers watching us closely.

Based on Yang's report I decide if we don't go now, we may never go. So, we decide, after all, to leave as planned on China Air ... and risk complete failure....

Our planned "scientific" testing model: "Don't Ask. Don't Tell!"

Yang Fan ... scout team extraordinaire.

Don't ask. Don't tell.

5.
Catching the Corpse...
The Singularity of Technology

"Science is the religion of
exploration in our times."

**This is a Renaissance imagination of what
CQ might have looked like.**

The government won't let us dig the site to prove Chinggis Qa'an (CQ) is buried on Mountain X in spite of our nine years of unique and historical research. Our expedition and investigations confirms our conclusion that this is the site of CQ's burial ground.

For years, we study technical equipment that can test what's beneath Mountain X without digging it up. Armies, archeologists and miners for their own reasons have and are developing tools to find what they are looking for below the surface. Such equip-

ment is expensive, often secret, and difficult to obtain and operate. True, even though the burgeoning field of geophysics is all about finding and identifying what is underground without digging.

We use magnetometry on the 2012 expedition to confirm the existence of major anomalies below Mountain X. We now need to discover whether the underground objects are consistent with our hypotheses CQ's grave is here. I'm sure this would be easier if we have the money, the security clearance, and the expertise to use the most advanced technology.

GSSI SIR 4000-Ground Penetrating Radar.

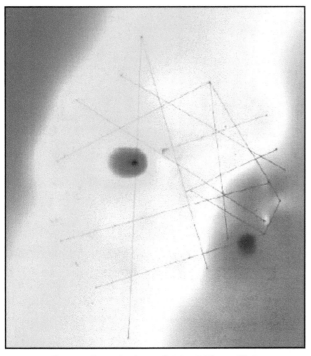
A two-dimensional plot of 2012 Expedition magnetometry results by Warren Caldwell, Stanford University doctoral student at the time.

Developer CEO of Mountain X provides our team a fancy lunch and tells us the story of "Buddha's Revenge."

But we must settle with what's reasonable: magnetometry, ground penetrating radar, walking surveys and open satellite imagery, each with its own sets of algorithms.

We consider but reject for various reasons an electronic resistance meter, a gravimeter, advanced metal detector, electronic molecular frequency discriminator, sonar, and muon radiography, at least for this expedition.

Can CQ and his family continue to outwit 800 years of exponential progress and expansion of the science of exploration and discovery?

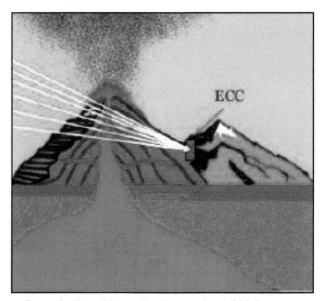
Cosmic-Ray Muon Radiography of Volcanos.

Advanced Metal Detector

6.
Magnetometry for Dummies...Like Me

"Magnetism from the center of the earth can tell our scientists what is 16 feet below us ... astounding singularity."

An artists pure imagination of what CQ looked like, but this version of CQ catches his spirit . . . tough and bright.

Archeologists, mineralists, cavers, treasure hunters, anyone who wants to see underground without digging or underwater without swimming uses magnetometry to "see" what's under the surface. In our last expedition in 2012, Warren Caldwell, who has a PhD in Geophysics from Stanford, used a magnetometer to detect metallic "anomalies" (something abnormal) under Mountain X.

For this Expedition we need more time to search, and better equipment, to test a broader area of the prescribed southeast side of Mountain X.

We accomplish our goal to test all the logical underground areas in 27 grids on Mountain X. This is thanks to our 2016 magnetometrist Jerry Griffith, our science team leader and former Silicon Valley executive, and Tim Leow from Livermore Labs, with the help of Becky Nichols and our medical

Magnetometry data survey ... Jerry and Tim.

officer Stew Lauterbach, M.D..

Jerry is specially trained by a Silicon Valley Company to operate the equipment. He also performs a minor miracle by finding the equipment we need in China so as to avoid shipping, customs questions and expedition-killing delays.

We bring home so much underground data that it will take months to analyze it. What will all those pretty pictures and columns of numbers show?

By measuring magnetic forces, we can determine if any metallic objects are underground and, with expert analysis, what those objects are. According to one vendor a magnetometer can find and identify a sword deep underground.

CQ was and still is a magnetized source of energy that, with analysis, will reveal the true "Secret of the Mongols."

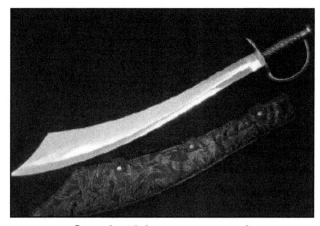

Sample 13th century sword.

9 White Temple center-mag

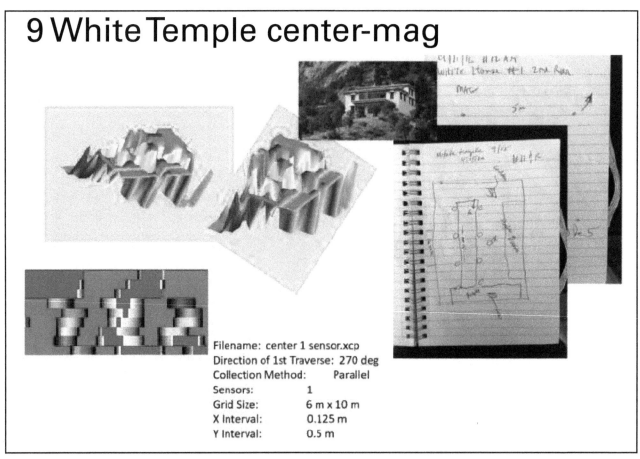

Filename: center 1 sensor.xcp
Direction of 1st Traverse: 270 deg
Collection Method: Parallel
Sensors: 1
Grid Size: 6 m x 10 m
X Interval: 0.125 m
Y Interval: 0.5 m

Sample plots and field notes from the magnetometry survey of the "White Temple Center," Grid 9, 2016

7.
The Joy of Penetration . . .
Ground Penetrating Radar (GPR)

"There's nothing like radar to find out what mother earth is hiding under her skirts."

This painter claims Chinggis Qa'an is thoughtful and introspective.

There's nothing as suited for penetrating our planet's earth as GPR (*Ground Penetrating Radar*).

Our GPR technical officer for science liaison is Tim Leow from the Livermore Labs in California, an internet and computer expert. I recruit him and the chief of magnetometry after a meeting of the local Explorers Club at Autodesk in San Francisco. He tells me he likes unsolved new technical puzzles. Our expedition certainly qualifies on that score!

He learns to operate GPR equipment with a company in Vermont and produces a "truckload" of underground data from Mountain X that our analysts will work on for the next few months. GPR is not limited like magnetometry to finding underground ferrous objects, but is a reflective beam that detects a variety of materials.

Stew Lauterbach, M.D., our medical officer

The GPR team in action on grid #11 ... "around the White Temple".

Thankfully a student technician comes with
our rented GPR. He and Tim set up
for the day's testing.

and scientist par excellence, helps the GPR Team, prepares the field notes and joins with Tim in gathering data. A Chinese GPR student also acts as Tim's assistant.

No matter what we find below the surface we know that Tim (GPR) and Jerry (Magnetometry) were 3-C Models: Competence, Concentration, and Conscientiousness ... whether we confirm the tomb of CQ or find something we never suspected ... like the tomb of CQ's grandson, Kublai Qa'an.

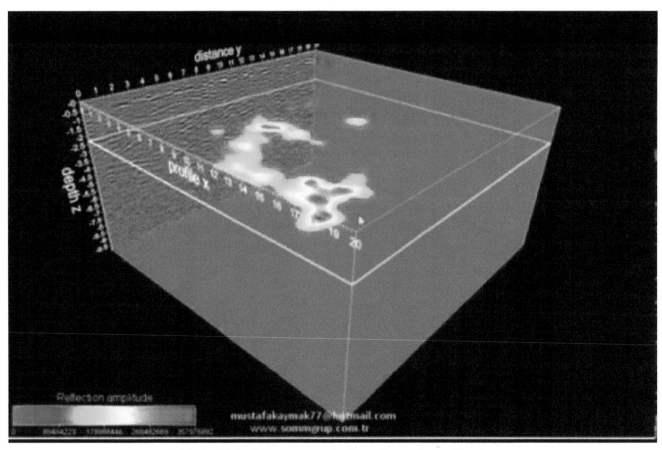

GPR Graphic 3-D test results in reflected amplitudes.

8.
Slow Boat to China ... And Slower Boat Home

"Use China customs at your own risk on the way to Ancient Mongolia."

A Westerner's imaginative picture of what CQ could have looked like ... cruel, withdrawn, deceptive.

Importing our technical equipment to China from United States can be a nightmare. Chinese Customs has a dangerous reputation, to say nothing of potential U.S. export controls on technical items.

We find out our GPR and Magnetometer do not require American export Customs approval but China has a history of confiscating, cannibalizing, delaying, overcharging customs, and making importing of technical products problematic. Do we dare take a chance to bring our equipment with our passenger baggage or employ a licensed importer?

If we guess wrong, our whole expedition is caput. We would have no chance to confirm technologically that Mountain X is where CQ is buried.

But thanks to Jerry we are able to lease the equipment in China and avoid the China Customs risks. Two Chinese agents, one part of a worldwide network and the other recommended by an American Company, say they will lease us what we need. Jerry's GPR source (a University professor) requires us to hire his student assistant to join us on the expedition to protect his machine; that student turns out to be most helpful. For that alone the extra cost is worth it.

But this approach has its complications. It takes weeks to recover our $16,000 deposit for the GPR that is "frozen" by the PRC Bank Regulators.

The equipment road block is resolved.

Now all the data is safely home. As the Mongolians would say: HOORAY!

On Mountain X above the tomb of Chinggis Qa'an

Science team Jerry & Stu with our Chinese magnetometer. The construction crane is helping to build a tram to the top of Mountain X and a huge Buddha ... for tourists, of course.

A Tibetan Mongol style rock cairn on the trail up Mountain X.

9.
Who Said Mountain X Was Sacred!!

"The vortex of my spirit and of the religions of our planet is the Sacred Mountain."

Living Mongols, especially in Ulaanbaatar, Mogolia's capitol, beleive Chinggis Qa'an looked like this ... strong and powerful.

We already confirm our site is in ancient Mongolia and that Mountain X is a Sacred Mountain.

How do I know our Mountain is sacred? It took me 239 pages in my 1979 book *"To Climb a Sacred Mountain"* to demonstrate in an around-the-world-journey how mountains become holy and stay that way for millennia. Such mountains are a "glimpse of the infinite, the true, the core."

Holy mountains are challenging visually and physically, enlightening mentally and

My Sacred Mt. Athos on the Aegean Sea is home to over 1000 Christian monks.

My Sacred Mt. Shasta, California. It is home to 200 different religions

My Sacred Mt. Kailas (Kangrinpoche), south west Tibet, where the earth and paradise meet.

My Sacred Mt. Fuji-san Japan. 400,000 pilgrims climb it every summer

My 1000 year old Daoist trails. *Above:* Hua Shan, China's Sacred Mountain of the West. *Right:* Mountain X, ancient Mongolia's Sacred Mountain of the East.

emotionally, and illuminating spiritually. They have a long and important history of relationships with our human spirit. Mountain X is no exception. Anyone who spends any time on this mountain "feels" its esoteric power. All our field team remark how strongly the mountain affects them ... and still does.

A traditional Tibetan monastery and Buddhist temple, in its Mongol form, existed here for over 350 years until destroyed in the 1960's. It is obvious that the sacredness of this mountain is understood before the temple is established; the holiness of the mountain site is the rationale for CQ's burial here.

In fact on a prior expedition a Mongol gives me a contraband photo from the 1950's of the Mongol Tibetan monastery that is hundreds of years old on Mountain X. It is torn down during the cultural revolution in the 1960s. Of course they build their monastery on their ancient and well known Sacred Mountain. It is a holy peak long before the time of Chinggis Qa'an (CQ).

The powerful head of the site development tells me a 40-day flood killed 129 peo-

ple including the leader of the Red Guards who destroyed the Temple. "Buddhist retribution," he says.

A small Han Buddhist temple still stands on the lower slope.

Intuition is an important source for understanding the special role of a Sacred Mountain as well as finding the tomb of C.Q.

I spent years, once China was open to foreigners, investigating, studying and climbing the five Daoist Sacred Mountains of China. Lao Tse, the legendary founder of Daoism, is credited with formulating that religion in the 6th century B.C.E. It was amazing to me how similar the only ancient remains on Mountain X, the trail to the summit, resembles the Daoist trails on these other Sacred Mountains in China, their location, construction and obvious identical design and "engineering."

Sacred Mountains always stand out in some way. They are instinctually as well as visually recognized on sight. My lifetime obsession with Sacred Mountains is why Professor Elverskog suggests I look for Mountain X. And why I recognize it's importance in the spirit worlds as soon as I see it the first time.

But it still takes me years of research and several expeditions to prove to others in absentia its special significance. Since everyone can't be on the mountain personally in our culture and times, others won't believe anything without "scientific" proof.

If you're not sure the mountain is sacred, don't take my word for it. Just visit it yourself. You'll know then Mountain X is a Sacred Mountain. And you'll be happier for the adventure to the spirit worlds.

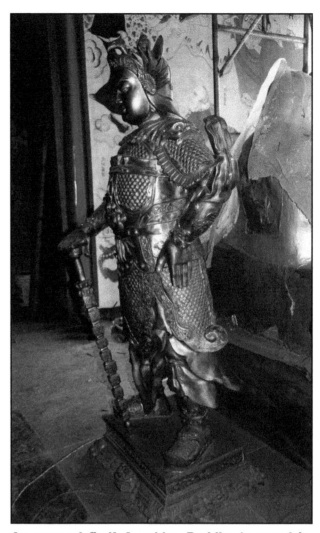

An unusual find! A golden Buddha (covered in plastic while repainting the temple) back to back with this warrior (CQ or his spirit) in the old Han Buddhist Temple at the bottom of Mountain X.

A sampling of of "my" other sacred mountains include: Machu Picchu (Peru); Arunachala (India); Maui (Hawaii); the sacred mountains of China; Mt. Sinai (Egypt); Omine-nan (Japan); Bumpess Hell at Mt. Lassen (California); Mt. Tabor (Israel), Mt. Kailas (Southwest Tibet).

Fly to catch the spirit of Mountain X — Hunnu Air.

10.
So What ... What's in CQ's Tomb

"Our mission in life tells us what's to be buried with us in death."

Unless we dig up his DNA, no one knows what Chinggis Qa'an looks like, but this is a typical Chinese idea, obviously influenced by Chinggis Qa'an's grandson Kublai Qa'an, founder of China's Yuan Dynasty.

Why have all those people including Marco Polo been looking for CQ's grave for over 750 years?

The *Secret History of the Mongols*, our years of research about CQ's life and his empire, along with an understanding of Mongol shaman burial practices, tells us what's buried with Chinggis Qa'an: The tools, people, implements, resources needed to carry out the mission assigned to him as a young man by his sky god Tengri (sometimes referred to as Otgon Uul Tenger) for both his temporal and afterlife. In Mongol spiritual tradition death is not the end of existence but merely a transition into another state, what we might call spirit.

CQ is buried with what he needs to continue to carry out his assigned mission, dead or alive, which is to protect his Mongolian people and "to bring the whole world under his sword." So, not just his bones will be in CQ's casket but also:

- Gold, silver, jewels, and precious metals.
- Armor, weapons, banners, flags.
- Remains of horses, camels, oxen with their equipage.
- Siege machinery, shields.
- Possible proclamations and other written materials in stone, metal, or even paper.
- Clothing, uniforms, packs.
- 78 crowns of conquered Kings.
- The remains of CQ: bones, hair,

nails, skull, skin.

- The human remains of servants, slaves, warriors, women and children.

- Works of art (functional or intentional).

- Religious and Shaman artifacts.

web archive

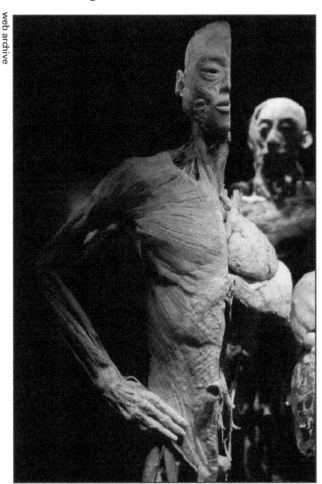

Dead men tell tales (DNA). Thanks to modern science CQ's tomb will be the best way to tell the world how he lived. (*Above*: a Mongol noble's skeleton, not CQ's)

In the Mongol empire you're free to pick your own Gods and religions, including Buddhism, Daoism, Christianity, Islam, Persian. Their artifacts may be buried with CQ.

Gold bracelet produced at Karakoram, once the capitol of the Mongol hegemony.

Silver coins, also produced at Karakoram.

Mongol warriors used animal hunting as training for warfare.
Hence, they could shoot arrows accurately backwards.

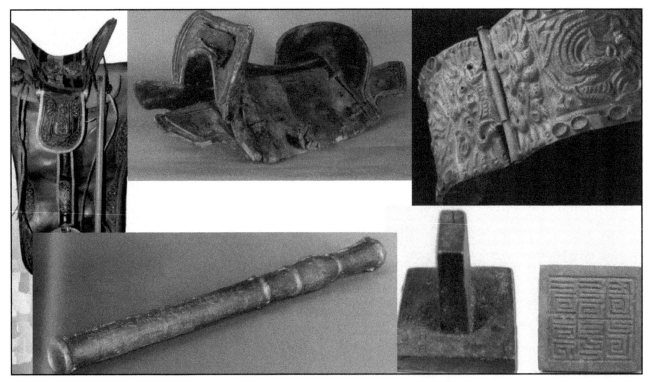

Mongol Empire artifacts.

11.
Revelations from the Dead ...
Grave Truths

"There is nothing like dying and being buried to let the whole world know about how you were living. It's the data that counts."

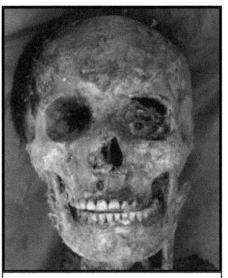

Overall we all look the same when we become skeletons. But today's scientists, based on CQ's tomb and skeleton, will tell us more than we can imagine about him and his Mongol Empire.

Gravesites are the source of incredible knowledge about people and cultures, thanks to the singular expansion of scientific knowledge and tools of analysis. We know so little about CQ, his conquests and civilization. His tomb will provide extraordinary insight into the world's greatest military commander and his empire, the largest in human history.

Why CQ dies is still a mystery, but his grave will also answer that question.*

Here are some samples of the revelations, both personal to CQ and about the broader culture of his world, that his grave will yield if the site is properly protected and analyzed by skilled archaeologists and other scientists:

Personal Findings About CQ
- injuries
- cause of death
- lifetime nutrition
- alcoholism
- hair and eye color
- mutations
- clothing

- health including dental
- personal weapons
- age
- longevity factors
- deformities
- disease
- comparative size
- height
- personal values as to
    - truth
    - knowledge
    - emotions
    - beliefs
    - family relationships
    - spiritual attitudes
    - beliefs

Findings About Mongol Culture
- food diet and nutrition
- religion
- clothing
- life expectancy and medicines
- classes and position in society
- social control and independence
- death rituals and practices
- warfare and weapons of warfare
- ingenuity in warfare
- manufacturing
- organization
- products
- artworks
- race
- genetics
- hair
- eye color and other information from ancient DNA analysis
- rules and regulations especially if writings are included
- strength and intelligence of warriors (particularly from size and complexity of weapons)
- treatment of and relations with animals, domesticated and wild
- money
- commerce

(Silk Web, Roman, Persian, Chinese products, for example)
- technology
- agriculture and industry
- effect on environment
- economics
- weather
- fears and anxieties, cultural and personal

That is an inkling of the knowledge we will gain. All such information and more is found from other gravesites by modern scientists.

All historical sources agree that CQ died after falling off his favorite horse Josoto Boro, while hunting. But there are many alternative theories as to what caused his fall: a fever; an infection; a disease, particularly malaria or typhus; an arrow shot in his thigh as reported by Marco Polo; a magic spell from his enemy the Tangut King; castration by his Tangut wife, or even lightening. In any event his death delayed the Mongol attack against the Tangut kingdom. War equipage undoubtedly also buried in CQ's tomb.

12.
Psycho-History of the World's Greatest Conqueror

"Look not to the battlefield but to the psyche to find the key to CQ's victories and to his grave."

The Secret History of the Mongols has no pictures of Chinggis Qa'an but, more importantly, gives us an understanding of his personality.

To some (particularly indigenous Mongolians) Chinggis Qa'an (CQ) is a "Saint" and to the rest of the world including "Europeans, Russians, Indians and "Persians", who were conquered, or were afraid they would be conquered, he is a brutal, vicious, bloodthirsty, tyrannical maniac, to say the least.

But who was CQ ... really?

Secret History

While *The Secret History of the Mongols* — a book of poetry and prose about Chinggis, his life, his family and his empire — is recognized as a most important source of what little knowledge we have on CQ and his

times, most scholars and writers ignore the psychological personal value of this work. It is generally agreed it was written during CQ's life, or between 3 and 30 years after CQ's death. This History is basically accurate, but admittedly a semi propaganda effort to make CQ "look good" according to his contemporary criteria of admiration.

Psychoanalysis

Even though I've read extensively in the field and was personally psychoanalyzed by Dr. Herbert Lehman years ago, those experiences and interests don't qualify me to psychoanalyze Chinggis.

Even Freud specifically recognizes purely

historical figures can't be psychoanalyzed. See his psycho histories of Leonardo da Vinci and Woodrow Wilson.

My note here is only to analyze the psycho-history of CQ based on the *The Secret History of the Mongols.* Anyone can make their own analysis of the details of CQ's psyche based on the outline following of CQ's psychic events with page and book numbers from *The Secret History.*

Boyhood — The Murder

CQ's birth name is Temujin. His father, a tribal leader, is poisoned by Tartar enemies when Temujin is about nine. After his father's death, his family (mother, daughter and 3 sons) are expunged from the tribe — a death sentence in those times and areas in Mongolia. CQ's youth is traumatic, deprived, dangerous and isolated.

A boyhood murder is a powerful part

of Chinggis Qa'an's inner life. He and his brother kill another half-brother who tries to dominate the family. Their mother is furious at Temujin, *"Why can't you work together when we have no friends but our shadows and no whip but our horses tails".*

CQ survives his early years of hardship, deprivation, isolation, capture and even enslavement because of his ingenuity, perseverance, willpower and family working together. Survival and ambition set the stage for his extraordinary accomplishments.

Mother / The Feminine

His mother ("clever, brave, high-minded, noble, wise, lawful" according to the *Secret History)* keeps the family alive with wild berries and roots until Temujin and his brothers are old enough to hunt.

In later years, he admits being afraid of his mother, an obviously powerful woman. This is an important psycho-clue.

The feminine influence on CQ must have been strong. His first "primary" wife Borte plays a prominent part in his life. He marries innumerable women, some of whom are valued advisors and profit personally and greatly from Chinggis' military successes. According to legend his Tangut wife castrates Chinggis with blades hidden in her vagina in revenge for his slaughter of her people, the Tanguts.

Father / The Masculine

Since his father dies when he is a young boy we have nothing to gauge the strength of his oedipal conflicts or his passive/ aggressive attitudes towards his father; yet murdering his older brother, outcasting family members, accepting his bastard son, and weeping for his sacrificing followers could well be explained by unconscious relations with his fatherly memories.

Chinggis is close to his father. His father selects Borte from another tribe for Ching-

Chinggis Qa'an's lifelong first wife, Borte.

Psychic Elements

We don't have enough information to analyze CQ's sublimations, repressions and identifications that he uses to live successfully and happily. We don't know if, in his view, he is even satisfied or content with his life. Like Sigmund Freud's analysis of President Woodrow Wilson, undoubtedly CQ's super-ego is never satisfied but always pushes him on, consciously and unconsciously, to conquer and govern more nations and peoples, to carry out his god's wishes and satisfy his fixations, to deal with his fear of his mother and the sight of blood, and his constant delegation to others to carry out his ordered punishments. Our inability to determine the demarcation between his conscious and unconscious actions and thoughts raise critical but probably unanswerable questions about CQ's psyche.

gis' future wife when Chinggis is about six years old. CQ honors that choice for the rest of his life (almost 60 more years).

Lineage

Temujin's long legendary lineage begins with "the blue-grey wolf." Like the Old Testament, Romulus, Jesus, Buddha and Moses, CQ's history affects his view of his own importance and obligations.

Libido/Super-ego

Although a classical analysis of CQ is impossible because of the lack of personal information, the *Secret History* of his outer life and vignettes from his inner reactions demonstrate an unusually strong libido and of course an overpowering super-ego. He continues his conquests and rules to his death at, for his times, a very old age (67).

CQ's narcissistic identification with his Sky God produces a lifetime of self-confidence.

CQ as a young man and prisoner locked in iron restraints.

He is strongly narcissistic but not illusory or psychotic. His ego and his character successfully balance his strong desire to win, to succeed, with his compassion for his family, his wives, his generals and warriors.

Revenge is one of CQ's strongest ideals and motivations. While it may seem immoral by our cultural standard, CQ's boyhood makes it understandable. CQ's culture is a revengeful society. Revenge is a moral concept of justice; it preserves and keeps the tribe together; it honors the memory of family members killed or hurt by outsiders (e.g. Chinggis' murdered father, his kidnapped wife, his slaughtered diplomatic delegation and the Tangut revolt). The threat of revenge can also scare away human predators.

The Secret History reports that CQ tells his servants every morning at breakfast to talk about killing the revolting Tanguts and say, "Maimed and tamed, they are no more."

Anyone understanding CQ knows that there will be drastic retribution for lying, disloyalty, abuse, injustice, murder, not doing one's duty, even violation of CQ's principles of diplomacy or laws and rules. Compassionate, generous, appreciative, rewarding, grateful, forgiving, competitive, determined are key characteristics and explain Chinggis' success with his army and conquered peoples. He values highly cooperation, direct communications, intelligence, companionship, perseverance, openness, honesty, and slavish dedication to CQ's mission and himself.

Personality

The Secret History is a treasure trove of vignettes about CQ's psycho-history. My summary below of excerpts with book and page numbers from *The Secret History* includes psychological information about Chinggis Qa'an: Parents and Childhood, Fratricide, Ancestors, Mother Power, Views of Spirit and heaven, Sorrow, Duties to Leaders, Revenge,

Choice, Compassion, Organization, Listening to Advice, Deception, Marital relations, Attention to Details, Disciplinarian, Delegation, Appreciation/ Rewards, Equality, Criminal Punishment, Principles, Communications, Personal Security/Fears, Gratitude, Competition, Forgiveness, Determination, and Loyalty.

Spiritual

CQ for his whole life identifies with his Sky God. He exempts priests from taxations and consults with spiritual representatives of many religions, particularly Daoist's. (A Dao priest Ch'ang-ch-un advises CQ that physical immortality is impossible.)

CQ adheres to the concepts and advice of his Mongol Shamans daily. He continually reminds everyone that his decisions and critical events are "heaven's will", not his own.

To CQ, Spirit, the 4th and most powerful dimension of energy, is beyond our physical, mental and emotional worlds. It is the way to God. CQ believes his spirit will ascend to God. Historians and scientists confirm that the spirit of CQ long outlives his physical death.

And in addition, his "spirit" carries over to this day, after his demise, particularly as to maintaining the secrecy of his tomb and his military plans to complete the conquest of Sung China.

Thanks to Chinggis' virility, his many wives and 32 generations, Chinggis' Y gene mutation carries over to 16 million male heirs in Central Asia. And his spirit is strong among the millions of his current Mongol devotees.

As to CQ's "spirituality" *The Secret History* reports his saying:

> *"Every morning I will*
> *sacrifice to Burkkhan*
> *Khaldun (CQ's holy*
> *mountain). Every day I will*
> *pray to it; the offspring of my*
> *offspring shall be mindful of*
> *this and do likewise.*

Smithsonian

A Mongol shaman's regalia.

Smithsonian

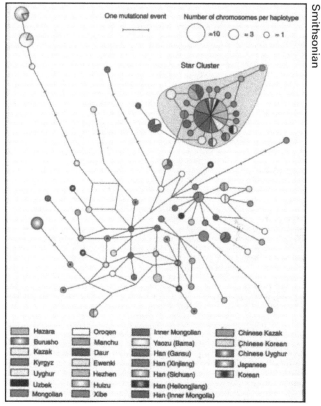

From *National Geographics* study
demonstrating sixteen million male heirs
of CQ who carry his mutation.

Extraordinary flexibility and mobility are keys
to the success of CQ's warriors.

This Pharaoh's mask
made of obsidian
likely traveled to
Karakoram all the
way from Egypt,
according to the cu-
rator of a traveling
exhibit about
Chinggis Qa'an.

Smithsonian

LAST WORDS OF
OF CHINGGIS QA'AN

"Know a man by his weapons,
His body by his teeth
His mind by his skull
His culture by his tomb
And his spirit by his horse."

We often see ourselves as others see us, or as we believe others see us. By that measure this is how CQ would see himself over the last 950 years. No one knows what CQ really looks like until his remains, his DNA, his structure are analyzed with modern science.

PSYCHO-FACTS REGARDING CHINGGIS QA'AN
FROM
The Secret History of the Mongols

What follows are "psycho-facts" about CQ taken directly from the most authoritative original (albeit translated) source, *The Secret History of the Mongols,* translated into English by Igor Rachewiltz in 2006 in two volumes including commentaries.

Each demonstrates the character, the personality, the ego of CQ. By reading them you can make your own conclusions as to the personality and psychological characteristics of CQ.

The book and page numbers from *The Secret History* are cited in parentheses.

■ Parents

CQ's childhood and youth is traumatic, deprived, poverty-stricken, isolated, and extremely difficult. His father is poisoned, his mother and family abandoned by his tribe (ordinarily a Mongol death sentence in those times). The tribe refuses to allow CQ and his family to stay with them for fear of being attacked by stronger tribes wanting to wipe out what is left of CQ's family.

■ Fratricide

CQ is allegedly abused by his brother who tries to "*boss*" CQ. In his anger CQ murders his brother. That earns him strong reproof from his mother.

■ Ancestors

The Secret History lists CQ's ancestors for many generations (much like the Old Testament) beginning with the *"blue grey wolf ".* CQ is obviously aware of this lineage. He always has a very strong bond with his family and its history, especially his father and later his wife and sons. (BOOK ONE, PAGE 1, 2.)

■ Mother Power Figure

CQ'S mother Ho-elim is abducted by CQ's father and later gives birth to CQ, their eldest child, his three bothers and one sister. (BOOK ONE. PAGE 59, 60). She personally chases down and castigates her husbnd's tribe for abandoning her and her sons after the death of her husband and CQ's father ... to no avail. (BOOK TWO, PAGE 74.)

She is, according to *The Secret History,* "*clever*" and nourishes and keeps alive her small children with wild berries and roots she digs. She is said to be "*brave*", "*high minded*", "*noble*", "*wise*", "*lawful*". (BOOK TWO, POEM AT PAGE 74, 75). She is outspoken in her criticism of her children. When the boys are fighting each other, she condemns them saying "*Why can't you work together when we have no friends but our shadows and no whip but our horses tail.*"

In a furor she objects to CQ's interrogation of one of her adopted sons about claimed disloyalty, based on statements to CQ by his long time friend, supporter and shaman Teb Tengerri. CQ, surprised by his mother's visit and complaint about CQ's alleged mistreatment of her adopted son, "*becomes afraid of her.*"

"*I was afraid of mother getting so angry and really became frightened and I felt shame and was really abashed.*" After he calms his mother, he later reduces the guilty sons status; his mother goes "*quickly into decline*." (BOOK TEN, PAGE 244.)

■ Spiritual

When very young he establishes his lifetime relationship with Tengri, the Mongol sky god and his mentor with whom he communicates atop the sacred mountain Burkhan Khaldun. E.G. (BOOK TWO PAGE 103.) When CQ avoids capture by hiding on this mountain he reports, "*I escaped with my life, a louse's. Fearing for my life, I climbed the Qaldun (sacred mountain). But I was greatly frightened.*"

Image of CQ doing obeisance to his SKY GOD Tengri. He shows humility by removing his hat, raises his arms, and hangs his belt around his neck.

When he escapes his enemies on the mountain, he says, "*Every morning I will sacrifice to Burkhan Khaldun, every day I will pray to it; the offspring of my offspring shall be mindful of this and do likewise."*

To do homage to his god he speaks and, facing the sun, hangs his belt around his neck, puts his hat over his hand, beats his breast with his fist, kneels nine times downwards to the sun,and offers a libation and prayer. (BOOK TWO. PAGE 103.)

■ Heaven

CQ regularly credits heaven for his successes. e.g., (BOOK EIGHT, PAGE 208.) "*I set out against the Sarta-ul people and protected by eternal heaven brought them into dust under submission."*

■ CQ Sorrows

"*Temujin (CQ's birth name) wept"* when he is told about his old family member who is wounded trying to force CQ's tribe not to abandon CQ, his mother and his siblings. (BOOK TWO, PAGE 73.) "*Tears fell from his eyes and his heart was pined"* on seeing a loyal warrior bleeding from his mouth from the fight. (BOOK SIX, PAGE 173.)

■ Duty to Leaders (aka Lords) ... Especially to CQ as a "Lord"

"*People who lay hands on their rightful lord must be cut down."* (BOOK FIVE, PAGE 149.)

CQ saves the lives of the men who fight against CQ's army so "*their lord could escape."* CQ does not kill these men but praises them as fighting men "*unable to forsake their rightful lord to enable their lord to escape."*

When one of CQ's leaders is killed in a battle, CQ gives his offspring the bounty given to orphans. (BOOK 6, PAGE 107.)

CQ has followers of an enemy leader executed for bringing their leader to CQ thinking they would be rewarded. "*Traitors to their lord"* he calls them. (BOOK EIGHT, PAGE 200.)

REVENGE... REVENGE... REVENGE...
A touchstone attitude for CQ and his culture in the 13th century.

■ Revenge

... a major impetus and rationale for CQ's actions and those of his armies.

CQ, after conquering his traditional Tartar enemies, states the purpose is to "avenge our fathers and forefathers. We shall measure the Tartars against the lynch pin of a cart and kill them to the last one." (Book Five, page 154.)

"*I shall set out against the Sartell people to take revenge, to requite the wrong for slaying my envoys."*

Revenge is key to CQ's war against the Tanguts in 1226-7. CQ orders his warriors:

"Kill the bold, kill the manly and the fine Tanguts, and let the soldiers take as many of the common Tanguts as they can lay hands on and capture." (BookTwelve, page 265.) He orders his troops to*"exterminate the Tangut people's mothers and fathers down to the offspring of their offspring, maiming and taming."* He says: *"While I take my meals you must talk about the killing and destruction of the Tangut and say, 'Maimed and tamed, they are no more.'"* (BOOK TWELVE, PAGE 268.)

■ Enemy Alternatives: Fight or Give Up

CQ can be trusted to do what he promises. *"If they oppose us, we shall fight them."* If they submit peacefully, CQ does not touch anything of theirs. (BOOK SIX, PAGE 176.)

■ Other compassions

CQ allows an old friend who becomes an enemy to be friends again, but at his friends request gives him proper burial without shedding any blood. (BOOK EIGHT, PAGE 201.)

■ Generosity

One of the reasons for CQ's success in recruiting warriors and leaders is his generosity in dividing spoils of battles and wars. (BOOK SEVEN, PAGE 187.)

■ Organization

CQ sets up his army in groups of 10s, 100s, 1000s, night guard, day guard, (sons and brothers of unit commanders). and details their operations. (BOOK TWO. PAGE 191.)

He appoints commissioners to govern conquered or subdued cities. (BOOK ELEVEN, PAGE 263.)

■ Listens and acts on good advice

(BOOK SEVEN. PAGE 193, 194.) (BOOK TEN, PAGE 242.) Upon advice of his commanders CQ *"ruffled as if he has smoke in his nose, then agrees and 'calmed down' and he spares the life of an accused traitor leader.*

After wife Yisui advises him to consider who would reign upon his death, CQ says. *"I would not follow the fore fathers. I slept as if I would not be caught by death."*

CQ is discussing who is to succeed him. All CQ's sons are asked their opinions. (BOOK ELEVEN, PAGES 244–246.)

■ Military Strategy

Deception and fear are strong aspects of CA's military and life strategies. See, for example, his battles with a rival large tribe the Naiman. (BOOK SEVEN PAGES 193–196.)

■ Wives

CQ has many wives in various levels of status from tribes and nations who give up peacefully or fight him. (BOOK SEVEN, PAGE 196.) *"CQ approves statement praising beautiful maidens. CQ "favors a wife and loves her ... and until the offspring of my offspring, they are not to abolish my wife Ibaqa's rightful place among my wives."* (BOOK EIGHT, PAGE 208.)

■ Attention to Details

CQ instructions and plans are very carefully thought out. For example, CQ gives detailed instructions to General Subetei for his invasion of enemy territory. CQ micromanages his night and day guards. (BOOK EIGHT, PAGE 199.) (BOOK NINE, PAGES 225-227.)

■ Strong disciplinarian and punishment

CQ orders beatings and even death for those who disobey. (BOOK EIGHT. PAGE 199.) He also orders punishment by Isolation and removal to far away places. *"Send them to a distant place out of our sight."* (BOOK NINE, PAGE 224.)

■ Delegates Leadership for Attacks, Wars, Military Action

. . . to Subetei (BOOK EIGHT, PAGE 199.), and to Jebe. (BOOK EIGHT, PAGE 202.) CQ gives orders to his "4 hounds." (BOOK NINE, PAGE 209.)

Smithsonian

Caracole Tactic

Enemy
Formation

Mongol line

40 -50 meters

Fires in Parthian fasion while turning

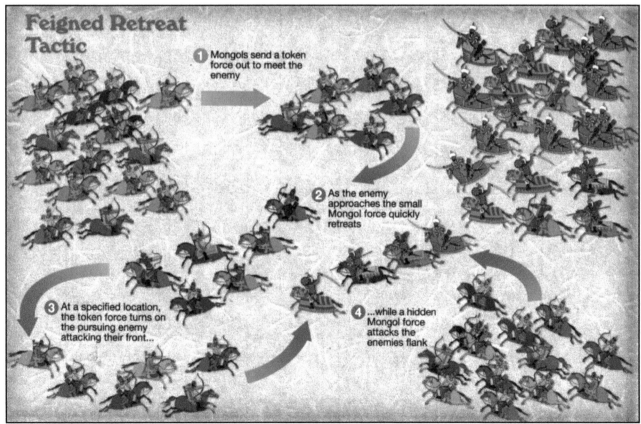

Feigned Retreat Tactic

1 Mongols send a token force out to meet the enemy

2 As the enemy approaches the small Mongol force quickly retreats

3 At a specified location, the token force turns on the pursuing enemy attacking their front...

4 ...while a hidden Mongol force attacks the enemies flank

CQ's tactics still taught and used in the world's military academies including West Point.

Smithsonian

CQ's success is based on the loyalty, stamina, and bravery of his warriors.

CQ sends his generals out on missions to conquer. (BOOK ELEVEN, PAGES 259-262.) He doesn't carry out his death sentences and punishments himself but orders subordinates to do it. He fears, as do most Mongls, seeing or touching blood, since that carries a persons dangerous spirit.

■ Equal treatment

CQ treats his adopted sons the same as his natural and even bastard sons, including a share of battle spoils . (BOOK EIGHT, PAGE 20.)

■ Crimes

CQ, consistent with tradition of the Mongols, punishes theft, lies, and adultery severely. (BOOK EIGHT, PAGE 20.)

■ Appreciation

CQ appreciates and doesn't forget past support and working together. CQ's actions to appreciate General Muquali and for military valor and success. (BOOK EIGHT, PAGE 206-208.)

■ Rewards

He gives generously the spoils of war to Commanders who fought with him before. (BOOK EIGHT, PAGE 20.) *"I shall now reward those among them who are most deserving."* (Not just family or tribe or for politics.) (Book Eight, page 203.) For giving good advice CQ excuses his generals from *"punishment for up to 9 crimes."*

CQ gives conquered people and even his wives to supporters, leaders, and family. (Book Eight, page 20.)

He pardons in advance *"up to 9 crimes"* both men and women followers. CQ shares hunting *"takes"* and war booty. He frees slaves. (BOOK NINE, PAGE 219.)

The night guards get the first food, drink, and female attendants. (BOOK TEN, PAGE 232.) Night guards are not committed to battles without a direct order from CQ. *"It is the night guards that watch over my golden life."* Guards are motivated to protect CQ by self-preservation, self-centeredness, egotism. They also control distribution of spoils,

48

food and act as judges. (BOOK TEN, PAGES 233-234.)

"*For victory I shall give him my daughter in marriage.*" But CQ requires gold, silver, pearls, silks as dowery. (BOOK TEN, PAGES 235, 238.)

Son Joci defeats the Forest People without fighting. CQ gives this people (the whole tribe) to Joci.

For defeating the Tumat people CQ gives his mother 10,000 people, his son Joci 9000 people, another Mongol leader 8000 people, an adopted son 5000 people, his son Tolui 5000 people and so on. (BOOK TEN, PAGE 242.)

Principles

CQ values and orders cooperation; straightforwardness; perseverance; openness and honesty especially with CQ; complete dedication like a "*slave*"; companionship; suffering together (wet and cold); equality of treating subordinates, (eg as to food and spoils); services to CQ (food and soup); killing Tatar enemies; and saving CQ's sons lives. (BOOK NINE, PAGES 212–214.)

Communications

CQ advises officers to communicate directly and not thru intermediaries, especially in dealing with CQ. (BOOK NINE PAGE 219.)

Commanders

CQ appoints several joint commanders, orders rewards and commands based on merit, and punishes severely. (BOOK NINE, PAGES 223-224.)

Personal security is vital to CQ

See night and day guards. Special privileges are provided for personal guards equal to those for commanders. Guards are equal rank with commanders. CQ orders strict rules with strong punishments for disobeying guards, or trespassing control area around CQ. (BOOK NINE, PAGE 229.)

Gratitude

CQ often expresses his thanks to his followers, especially the Night Guard. "*My elder night guard ... my true hearts night guards who in that swirling snow storm, in shivering cold, in pouring rain, taking no rest, stand all around my latticed tent bringing peace to my heart. You have made me gain this throne of joy*". (BOOK TEN, PAGE 230.)

Competition

When his Shaman, Teb, was disrespectful of CQ's family, CQ lets the family break the Shaman's back. CQ feels threatened by Teb followers. "*Because they laid hands on my younger brothers and spread baseless slanders among them in order to sow discord, he is no longer loved by Heaven in his life, together with his body, has been taken away.*" (BOOK TEN, PAGE 246.)

Forgiveness

Upon their petition CQ is appeased and allows the three sons into his presence but rebukes them quoting ancient words, citing old sayings, "*and reprimanding them to the point where they almost sank in the place where they stood, to the point where they could not wipe off the sweat of their brow.*" Quiver bearers advise CQ of the good points of his sons so "*appeased by these words, his anger abates*". (BOOK ELEVEN, PAGE 260.)

Determined

When advised to withdraw because he is sick and is challenged to fight by a Tangut leader, CQ refuses to withdraw saying "*when one lets oneself be addressed so boastfully, how can one withdraw.*" And he does not withdraw.

13.
The Hunter ... A Study in Hubris

By definition there's more hubris than objectivity searching for the gravesite of Chinggis Qa'an.

The Persian version of Chinggis Qa'an.

We do know Alan, the Hunter, inside out.

It's the height of hubris to compare myself, the Hunter, to Chinggis Qa'an, the Hunted.

It's admittedly my optimism to imagine that I could discover what Chinggis Qa'an and his family, history's recognized leaders in deceit, keep hidden for 798 years despite the efforts of hundreds of explorers, known and unknown.

CQ has the exaggerated self-confidence to think he can conquer the world and I'm just as overconfident to think I've found his secret tomb. If you're hunting panthers, you're a different species, but you may be the killed not the killer unless you have special interest, experience, knowledge, persistence, and even courage. I'm no Chinggis Qa'an but I know where his tomb is hidden.

What do the Hunter (Me) and the Hunted (Chinggis Qa'an) have in common or in contrast?

We both are lifetime warriors but in our own war cultures ... CQ, a military leader, me a volunteer warrior and a courtroom lawyer. We are similar in our ambitions to lead and govern, even though CQ is an immortal in human history and relatively no one ever hears of me.

Our life's works are completely different and my accomplishments minuscule (see Author Explorers Publications and Explorations in Postscript 11) compared to CQ's, but in many ways we are alike. We both are blessed with strong mothers, can concentrate obsessively, politically ambitious, energetic, long lived, secretive, strategic thinker. We also appreciate women, attract and delegate major responsibilities to loyal supporters, know the value of our team, strongly value cooperation, and grow up on our own with our peers, "our neighborhood." We have many values in common like positivity, cooperation, strong emotions, organization and detail, decisiveness, appreciation, gratitude, competition, forgiveness, and a strong sense of duty.

Throughout our entire lives CQ and I are oriented to the spiritual aspect of our exitance. Particularly in our later years we become aware of the opportunities of longevity, the internal governance of our energies, and the worlds beyond our physical, mental, and emotional selves. Yet CQ is much more closely related to his Shaman than I ever am to any priest.

And while CQ could never read or write, we both value the written word. As a lawyer and an author, I spend my entire life immersed in writings and words. CQ creates a whole new language and literature, to say nothing of detailed rules and regulations to govern his empire.

Probably because of the issues of survival in the 12th-13th century in Asia, CQ not only murders his own brother and innumerable enemies but is consumed for his entire life by his thirst for revenge.

As a young boy I recognize similar emotions in fights, games, and competitions —

CQ's Family Tree of warriors/rulers.

National Geographic

"kill the bad guys" — in sports, boxing, politics and wars — but the urge to kill is overcome by the laws, morals, and cultures of my times. On the other hand, CQ's obsession with his own personal safety and protection (with his Night and Day guards, for example) has no practical basis for my life in my times.

CQ's generosity and system of rewards and punishments are much better identified and practically activated than my own more emotional/ mental support for those working with me.

And while CQ activated commercial trade along the Silk Web (aka erroneously "Silk Road") more than ever in history, my only claim of interest is to be the first person in history to ride bybicycle the Silk Web from Istanbul, Turkey to Xian, China, the old capitol.

On the surface CQ and I have nothing whatsoever in common. But human potential and possibilities should never be underestimated...There are times in history when "Nobodies" overcome the efforts and objec-

The spiritual arbiters of the inner life . . . Jesus for our culture, the Shaman in ancient Mongol culture.

**Alan at small Han Temple on Mountain X with gold statues
of Buddha back to back with a warrior.**

14.
The Hunt ... A Study in Perseverance

"Dead spirits can kill or inspire you."

This artist thinks Chinggis Qa'an has a sense of humor.

know CQ is buried on Mountain X in ancient Mongolia in 1227. The world will know when it is confirmed by advanced underground technology including magnetometry, ground penetrating radar and satellite imagery or at least when permission to excavate is granted.

For almost 800 years people try to find the tomb of CQ and fail. My close analysis of the history of CQ during his last 30 days of life confirms he must be buried on a Sacred Mountain within cart range of the Liu Pan Mountains where he dies. Consistent with Chinggis Qa'an's family's masterful deception, CQ's actual gravesite is unknown and unsuspected until now. Only in Mountain X could CQ carry on his afterlife mission to protect his people and bring the rest of the world, especially Sung China, under his sword as prescribed by his Sky-God and his Mongol Shaman.

Here's the CQ's burial story of deception, Shaman death rituals, and history.

CQ dies in the Liu Pan mountains in August 1227.

CQ honors and accepts the burial precepts of Mongol Shamanism and Mongol tribal traditions: very importantly Mongol shamen recognize the extreme dangers and evil spirits occupying a corpse; the corpse must not be touched, talked about or visited except under very restricted Shaman-prescribed conditions.

- A dead body must be buried as quickly as possible.
- CQ must be buried on a Sacred Mountain inside ancient Mongolia.
- CQ's corpse must be transported by cart from his place of death to his gravesite by a fast and feasible route.

53

Alan and Becky next to a tree that the locals claim (mistakenly) grew up over CQ's grave site.

Everyone thought CQ's silver casket was on a cart like this so they missed the cart with the wooden casket and CQ's real remains.

- CQ and his followers believe the Spirit of a deceased person is extraordinarily powerful.

- CQ must still carry on his god-given mission even after his death.

- CQ desires, and his surviving family is obliged, to conceal the grave of CQ, and do so.

Consistent with CQ and his family's military genius based on deception, the site of CQ's burial is not only concealed but the world is deceived into believing he is buried in northern Mongolia near his birthplace and his special Sacred Mountain Burkhan Khaldun. Wooden and silver caskets are switched to accomplish the misdirection (in magician's terms) so as to deceive those personally in his 75-cart funeral cortege including its 2,500-warrior guard force.

After 40 years of studying and hiking on Sacred Mountains, I investigate and explore many Mongolian Sacred Mountains and the alternate claimed burial grounds of CQ— northern Mongolia, Karakoram, battlefields, forests, rivers, Liu Pan. These sites have been explored for over 750 years and in recent years using the most sophisticated and advanced technologies.

Mountain X is the only mountain that satisfies the historical, geopolitical, and spiritual requirements for the grave of CQ.

The reason the grave-site has never been found until now is because everyone has been looking in the wrong place!

The Liu Pan Mountains—CQ's death site. Note bottom right, the road beginning of the route of his cortege to his Mountain X burial site.

15.
The Way of the Disappearing Corpse

"For the dead man and our story, it's not where you die but where you lie that's important."

Here is an oft used painting of Chinggis Qa'an as a Chinese Daoist sage.

In 1227 Chinggis Qu'an's (CQ'S) Family and his shaman cart his dead body from the Liu Pan Mountains to his Mountain X gravesite, for 798 years one of the best kept secrets in history.

My first hint and knowledge of CQ's missing tomb site comes from Professor John Elverskog's insight that according to Mongol shamen corpses are dangerous and full of evil spirits. Hence CQ's corpse must be disposed of and interred as promptly as possible consistent with Mongol burial practices.

The "Secret History of the Mongols" is silent on the whole subject of CQ's death other than asserting *"he ascended into heaven".*

Since CQ dies in Ningxia and must be buried in ancient Mongolia, our expedition must prove a feasible speedy route for CQ's funeral cart. My original thinking proves erroneous. The original cortege couldn't have

The casket was empty since CQ "ascended into heaven" along the way.

55

traveled my proposed way in any reasonable time. But in this expedition we do discover the route used. (See map below prepared by reporter Tessa Chan based on her interview with Alan Nichols.)

Some of the historical and legendary clues that lead us to the route of the funeral procession include: CQ's silver casket is empty when the shaman opens it at Burkhan Khaldun in north Mongolia according to the

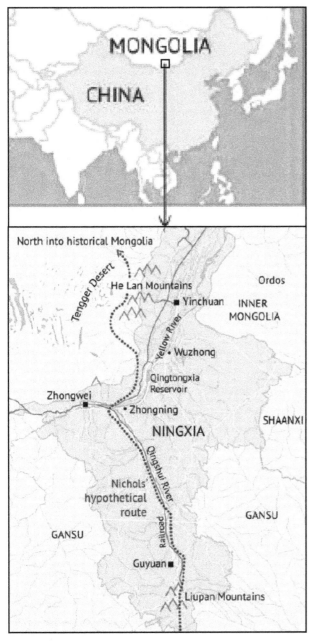

The way of the Disapearing Corpse from the Liu Pan towards Mountain X (from a map prepared by SCMP based on the reporter's interview of Alan the Hunter).

research of Italian scholar Erdeni Tobchi. If CQ did not actually "ascend into heaven", he must be buried on the way to north Mongolia.

According to another Italian academician there are two caskets, one silver and one wood. Like all magician's misdirection, one casket you notice and see; one casket, you don't. Everyone in the cortège, including the guards and servants, believe CQ's corpse is in the wrong casket and in the wrong cart.

Any person not an official part of the funeral cortège who sees any of the carts of the procession is immediately executed by the horse guard of from 800–2500 warriors.

Camels, rather than oxen or horses, are most likely to be used to pull the death carts because of their speed and stamina.

The carts take direct and level roadways as are available. (CQ's armies prior to CQ's death use these same valleys and plains during military operations against the Tangut and the wars against the Jin in north China).

Speed is most important so the funeral procession travels by day and night and avoids swamps and rivers, mountains, sand, rugged topography and populated areas, where possible.

Since CQ while alive is in this area of Mountain X during his campaigns, he may very well pick his own gravesite. It is reported that Mongol nobles, while they live, often select their own place to be buried.

John Man, author of *Genghis Khan... Life, Death, and Resurrection,* reports from Sagan's *History of the Eastern Mongols and their Royal House,* "a clue to the route of the funeral cortege is an incident in the area where the death cart with CQ's casket is stuck irremovably in the mud. In the night CQ's son dreams CQ tells him "Bury me here". They do ... on Mountain X. Author Man goes on to relate, "The cortege would probably be heading east to join the route covered so many times by Genghis against the Jin (the north Chinese)."

16.
Dreaming on Mountain X ...

"There can be no discovery without dreaming."

Without a mirror, we can't see ourselves, especially what's behind us.

Sharing the knowledge and the wisdom we discover is the essence of this expedition and all exploration. Otherwise it's a waste of time.

How are we disseminating our findings? Presentations and videos, television, print and e-book, Technical Article White Paper, Media (Past and Future), Podcasts, the internet, and Advisor Reports.

I develop my own spiritual, mental, and physical consciousness from a lifetime immersion into my own spirit and on Sacred Mountains all over the world, involving innumerable current and ancient religions. This extraordinary venture begins with my 40-day expedition around the world recounted in my book, *To Climb a Sacred Mountain ... One Man's Search atop the Sacred Moun-*

Sacred Mountains inspire our secret worlds.

Sages, Bodhisattvas, Wise men, Yogi ... the spirit of enlightenment.

tains of the World. This expedition to find the tomb of CQ grows out of my findings that CQ (like Mongol princes) is buried on a Sacred Mountain.

This in turn raises the story of my sharing for the first time in my life my own personal living truths, my spirit keystones, my "Who am I".

I am spending a night in my sleeping bag on the ground at the entrance to the Tibetan temple being built on Mountain X. I wake up around 4:30 in the morning. The head of our video/TV team Caleb Sappola, to my surprise, is already "in the dark" setting up his equipment for the day's shoot. He proceeds to film my entire daily "contemplation" of over 125 concepts, my "living truths," to live and die by ... set in the glory of a sunrise on our holy Mountain X.

It is the first time in my life I contemplate aloud my daily precepts with someone listening. Come to think of it, it's no surprise to me that a Sacred Mountain, Mountain X, opens me up as never before ... in the underworld spirit of Chinggis Qa'an where he is buried.

Although many of the concepts were part of my psychoanalysis with Dr. Hert Lehman in my 40's, they are the product of 87 years of deciding "Who am I".

If you're interested, my own "Living Truths" follow.

Jigoku and the living truths at
sunrise on Mountain X.

... The Living Truths

The future is in our dream.

Who Am I ...The Hunter

These precepts are who I am, metaphorically, my immutable empty cup to be filled with my life experiences, intentional or unconscious. This expedition fills my cup to the brim. It is a failure unless our journey adds something positive to your, the reader's, life-cup.

My Precepts are Divided Into Four Categories ...

... Jigoku

From my Shugendo experience on Japan's Sacred Mountain Omine-san, meaning the negatives that make me unhappy.

... My Living Truths

The positives that reactively or proactively bring me happiness.

... The Ten Steps to Shugendo Happiness

... The Tools To Find Myself

... Meditation ... Contemplation ...
... Introspection ... Prayer ...

Each word that follows relates to important thoughts and experiences for me ... hopefully to the reader, you.

JIGOKU TO UNDERSTAND MY UNHAPPINESS
My Negatives

- Anxiety
- Greed
- Guilt
- Grief
- Regrets
- Poor Me Attitude
- Ill Will
- Envy/Jealousy
- Hate
- Anger
- Lust (except for sex)
- Hubris
- Depression
- I-Centeredness
- Selfishness
- Judging myself by what I think others think of me
- Overreaction to Criticism
- Obsession with Praise
- Pride
- Bragging
- Resentment

MY LIVING TRUTHS
My Positives That Make Me Happy and Who I Am

- Love
- Joy
- Peace
- Harmony
- Quietude
- Appreciation
- Appreciation of Beauty
- Gratitude
- Solitude
- Communion
- Generosity
- Self Love (privately)
- Compassion for the Suffering
- Compassion for the Happiness of Others
- Justice
- Familiarity
- Forbearing
- Forgiving
- Kindness
- Trust
- Equanimity
- Here
- Now
- Aware of God (the Force of Happiness)
- Submit to God
- Connect to God
- Bodhisattva
- Wisdom
- Awe
- Reverence
- Patience
- Mindfulness
- Positiveness
- Courage
- Humility
- Humor
- Detachment
- Comfort
- Contentment
- Conscience
- Consciousness

- Concentration
- Confidence
- Honesty
- Transparency
- Sociability
- Friend-ability
- Intimacy
- Cooperation
- Dynamics of the living truths
- Proactive/Reactive
- Discovery
- Dissemination
- Discernment of Truth
- Discriminating Decisions
- Discipline
- Determination
- Imagination
- Creativity
- I Am That I Am
- I Am That I Think I Am
- I Am the Universe
- Middle Path
- I Am In Nirvana / I Am Nirvana
- Yin/Yang
- The Mountain More Than The Summit
- Time (Relative/ Precious)
- Health (Physical, Mental, Emotional Spiritual)
- The Living Truths Assuage, Cure, Prevent Disease
- All Is Impermanent and/or Permanent
- Entanglement
- Emptiness
- Cause/Effect
- Is Is Best
- I Am It
- Let It Flow
- Let Go
- We'll See
- Just This Is It
- The Tao

- Nature
- Natural
- Holiness of Light
- Holiness of Sound
- God Is Mystery
- Spirit Is The Way To God
- Spirit Is Energy
- Spirit Fourth Dimension
- Bodhisattva
- Time, Energy, Means, Health, Desire – The Way To Enlightenment

THE TEN STEPS TO SHUGENDO HAPPINESS, YOURS AND MINE
BODHISATTVA

- Jigoku
- Survival
- Rebirth
- Cooperation
- Death Consciousness
- Transitory / Transparent
- Power/Transformation
- Power/Transcendence
- 360 Degree Vision
- Right Thought/ Right Talk/ Right Action
- Who Am I
- Here, Now, Mindfulness, Positivism, Service, Bodhisattva
- Happiness/ Laughter
- Nirvana

17
Its The Team, Not The Explorer

"CQ's victories and our Expeditions' discoveries are illusions transformed into realities thanks to THE TEAM."

We may honor and admire explorers like Chrisopher Columbus, John Glen, Dr. David Livingston, Admiral Richard Byrd, Lewis and Clark, Tensing Norgay, or Charles Lindbergh. But None of them discovered anything, nor could they have succeeded, without a team. That's also true with all our four Chinggis Qa'an (CQ) tomb expeditions in ancient Mongolia.

And among the teams on this expedition are some very special Explorers pictured above:

1. **Geoffrey Gray,** Director Media Production and owner and Founder of True.Ink
2. Technical (**Tim Leow** and **Jerry Griffith**) and Logistics (**Becky Nichols**) Field Team with local housing and food team;
3. **Damien De Loup, Ph.D.**, China operations and archeological advisor, Archeology Consultant;
4. **Johan Elverskog, Ph.D.**, Academic patron of expedition and originator of search for tomb of CQ, Professor and Author, Southern Methodist University;
5. Television and photo media team led by **Caleb Seppala**, Team Leader and internationally known photographer, and **Jackson McCoy,** Sound Director and expedition philosopher, with local support staff.
6. **Yang Fan**, Local coordinator, expedition scout, and Founder and Owner of Beijing Venture Capital Firm
7. **Tessa Chan**, Newspaper reporter imbedded in expedition, and Journalist for the South China Mountain Post
8. **Tsung Shen**, Historical advisor and trans-

lator, Retired Professor from China's most prestigious science university and in the United States Massachusetts Institute of Technology (M.I.T.)

9. **Njambi Mungai**, CEO Sponsor Sacred Mountain Foundation, Founder and Owner J.R. Lester and Associates

10. **Mark Weiman**, CFO Sponsor Sacred Mountain Foundation, Founder and Owner Regent Press

11. Sponsor **Frederik Paulsen**, Owner and Chair of Ferring Pharmaceutical, Special Advisor to President Putin of Russia, internationally recognized Polar Explorer, philanthropist, Honorary Director of the the Explorers Club, and founder of our sponsor, the Mamont Foundation

12. **Zhu You Jia**, Stanford graduate student, writer and expedition Chinese language translator.

13. Living Statues and Science Team left to right:

    a. **Stew Lauterbach, M.D.**, Expedition Medical Officer and Magnetometry and GPR data team, Emergency Physician

    b. **Tim Leow,** Ground Penetrating Radar Director and Research Scientist at Livermore Labs

    c. **Jerry Griffith,** Chief Scientist and Director of magnetometry, Retired Executive of Silicon Valley companies.

14. **Dr. Simon Klemperer,** Expedition Science advisor and Professor of Geophysics Stanford University.

Not shown separately:

15. **Becky Nichols** (in picture 2), Expedition operations, Logistics for 4 Explorers Club Flag Expeditions in Bhutan, Turkey/Iran, China, Mongolia, and Tibet.

16. **Michelle L. Wright,** Expedition financial officer, Founder and owner of accounting firm "Michelle L. Wright CPA"

17. Vendors and Providers including GSSI (Geophysical Survey Systems, Inc./ Peter Leach), Geometrics (Kevin Harvey): pilots, drivers, suppliers, bankers, instrument rental (Beijing Eusci Technologies Ltd.), **Nicholas Tripcevich** (UC Berkeley Lab Manager), **Scott Byram** (Magnetometry Consultant)

18. Special events hosts for Beijing dinners including **Nebo Huang,** China billionaire poet, **Yang Fan,** and the developer CEO of the Spiritual Park site on Mountain X.

Our Beijing dinner host Nebo Huang and his assistant.

True.Ink Production Team

Their competence, dedication, and energy inspire me. Their interviews were extraordinary. They are the first up and the last to stop each day so they could capture the expedition in the best lights. They open me up to discover who am I and why I'm so obsessed with finding the tomb of CQ.

The team creates 80 hours of outstanding still and video photos that are being boiled down to one hour or half an hour at most! No one except video editors will have the time to see it all.

As long as I live (...and maybe beyond!) I will feel blessed and inspired by Caleb's video archive of his questions and my spirit answers on Mountain X in the Tibet temple.

True.Ink production team.

The credit for our success in this last expedition, as in the others, is thanks to four groups: Sponsors, Field Team, Core Team, and Special Advisors listed below as Expedition Explorers.

EXPEDITION EXPLORERS

Ross Anderson
Jennifer Arnold
Robert Ashton
Robert Atwater
Burt Avedon
Mumtaz Ay
Guitty Azarpay
Joe Bachheller
Bob Ballard
Dr. David Baltimore
Brittany Barbezat
Helen Barrera
Michael Barth
Wright Bass
Morton Beebe
Joan Linn Bekins
Jan & Julia Bender
Daniel Bennett
Raena Bennett
Barbara Berg
Megan Berkle
Giacomo Bernardi
Josh Bernstein
Kevin Binkert
David Black
Richard Blake
Sharyn Blaney
Worth Blaney
Ethan Blau
Rob Bolt
Leo Le Bon
Brian Boom
Barry Boothe
Joan Boothe
Sarah Bouckoms
Ben Bourgeois
Pete Bowser
Yulia Boyle
Jeff Bradley
Lawrence Brahm
Christopher Bray
Helen Breck
Sheldon Breiner
Larry Briggs
Harry Brooks
Rodney Brown
Christopher Buckley
Charlie Buffet
Duncan Burke
Louise Burrill-Geraci
Warren Caldwell
Kevin Callaghan
Mimi Calter
Martha Campbell
Teresa Cardoza
Celia Carey
Hugo Castello
Tessa Chang
Will Chang
Amy Charmosa
Julianne Chase
Karma Choeda
Laurel Chor
Christina Christensen
Nick Clinch
Vincent Colegrave
David Colleen Leof
Jonathan Conrad
David Conte
Catherine Cooke

Mauricio Coronado
Dave Cowan
Heather Creighton
Tom Cromwell
Fernando Cruz
Don Dana
Paul Danneo
Tom Davey
Randy Dean
John Dema
Kevin Denlay
Albert Dien
Constance Difede
Michael Diggles
Judy Dodge
David Dolan
Gerard Donovan
Karma Dorji
Jason Dunn
Susan Dutcher
Sylvia Earle
Carlos Echevarria
Jim Edwards
Farouk El-Baz
Kenton Elliot
Johan Elverskog
Timothy Emanuels
Ken Emmer
Caroline Ergetie
Kathleen Erickson
Sue Estey
Leslie Ewing
Justin Faggioli
Alva Falla
Yang Fan
Samantha Fargeon
Greg Farrington
Alan Feldstein
Dave Fickbohm
David Field
Doug Finley
Neil Fiske
Lacy Flint
Nancy Forester
John Fortune
Kay Foster
Mark Fowler
Paul Freitas
Joseph Frey
Debra Friedkin
Mark Friedman
Max Gallimore
Jean Ganza
Richard Garriott
Victoria Garshnek
Jim Gehrmann
Fred Gellert
Don George
David Gething
Fabricia Girardeau
Ronald Glantz
Milke Goldstein
Frank Gordon
Kristina Gossman
Lindsey Grant
Geoffrey Gray
William Grayson
Jerry Griffith
Brooke Grindinger/
Nichols

Gert Grobler
Dean Gushee
Les Guthman
Mark Hamilton
Brian Hanson
Karen Hawkes
Richard Hempsell
Andrew Herkovic
Robert J Higgins
James Ho Wong
William Holman
Kelley Hood
Leslie Hook
Lincoln Howell
Ken Howery
Andrew Hoyem
Mike Huang
Wade Hughan
Arnaud Humbert
Jerry Hume
Kevin Hurley
JM Hurson
Von Hurson
Jack Jensen
Fred Johnson
James Johnson
Alan Jones
David A Jordan
Debora Kalmon
Peter Kampf
Randy Katz
Steven Killpack, MD
Simon Klemperer
Michael Max Knobbe
Dida Kutz
Sharon Kwok Pong
Lee Langan
Oliver Langan
Stew Lauterbach
Sarah Lazarus
Peter Leach
Verna Lee
Hayne Leland
Damien Leloup
Mord Lewis
Albert Lin
Edward Lipman
Bill Liss
Timothy Loew
Gavin Magdycz
Orville Magoon
Bob Mallot
Haig Mardikian
Cary Martin
Peter Mason
Stephanie Mason
William Matthews
Tamara Mazur
Ed Mc Nulty, M.D.
Nini Charles McCone
Jackson McCoy
Bill & Brenda McKown
Howard C Mel
Marco Meniketti
Gregory Deyer Menjian
Don Miller
Robert Miller
Marvin Morgenstein
Marguerite Moriarty
Bill & Eva Marie Morrish

Rich Morrison
Jeff Morshead
Michael Moser
Michael Moyer
Toby Mumford
Njambi Mungai
Emerald Nash
Marston Nauman
Call Nichols
Lindsey Wilson Nichols
Shan Nichols
Sharon Nichols
Tucker Nichols
Max Nichols
James Nobles
Warner North
Maria Orth
Frederik Paulsen
Malcom Potts
Matthew Prior
Stan Prusiner
Ryan Pyle
Brian Ramsey
Jonathan Reisman
Joan Ring
Will Roseman
Elizabeth Rosen
Sylvia Rossa
Becky Rygh
Charlotte Rygh
Rick Saber
Hank Saroyan
Steven Schwankert
Stan G Scott
Caleb Seppala
Scott Setrakian
Andy Shaw
Tsung Ying Shen
Anne Simpson
S.E. Smith
Samuel Sperry
Eric Stackpole
Carol Staiger
Judy Stark
Marc Stolman
Isaac Stoner
Don Stow
Norbu Tenzing
Po Tong
Nichols Tripcevich
Clarence Tsui
Kirk Usher
Alan Valdes
Edward Van Porten
Rosemary
Vandenbroucke
Marie Vanek
Peter Vestal
Herman Wanf
Mark Weiman
Harriet Weller
Dede Whiteside
Mike Wiedman
Jeff Wilson
Lindsey Wilson
Douglas Woodring
Michelle Wright
Lu Xu
Alyssa Young

EXPEDITION POSTSCRIPTS

A Spirit First: Circumambulating Mountain X

20.11
Post Magazine

24 LOOKING FOR CHINGGIS
The location of Genghis Khan's burial site is an 800-year-old mystery that has captured the imagination of explorers and scholars alike.

24
"He's a Mongolian leader and there's no way you'd bury him in China. So the point now is to track how he got [back to ancient Mongolia] – nobody's actually established that before."
—Explorer Alan Nichols

Alan and his camel friend search the Gobi in vain to track the way of "the disappearing corpse".
(Photo, Tessa Chan, SCMP)

POSTSCRIPT I

Chinggis Qa'an Prior Expedition Flag Report from 2012

Report on Flag 186 Expedition "Dead Men Tell Tales...The Last Days of Chinggis Qa'an.
Inner Mongolia, Ningxia.
Dates: September/October, 2012

The Team

The Field Team:

      Paul Zhang, Translator and locals coordinator

      Mike Pizzio, Security and Transport

      Warren Caldwell, Stanford Geophysics Testing (Magnetometry)

      John Rice, Conde Nast Producer

      Hira Hitachi, Videographer

      Tim Cleary, Production/Sound

      Damien Leloup, China Institutional Contacts and Archeologist advisor

      Steven Schwankert, China Flag and Public Relations

Special Advisors:

      Lee Langan, Originator of Magnetometry measurement techniques

      Sheldon Breiner, Academic and Equipment Adviser

      Professor Peter Kemperer, Geophysics, Stanford

Advisers: over 45 persons who provided special support and advice

Expedition interviewees at local sites:

      Vice Mayor of the nearby Mongol Village, mountain site park staff, local Lama and his nephew, Buddhist Nun, Mausoleum "tomb watchers" and their supervisor, Yinchuan gravesite official, ranger and administrator of Liu Pan Park, many locals at the Tomb site and equipment providers at Hohhot.

Summary

The purpose of this expedition is to track the last days of Chinggis Qa'an (C.Q.) in 1227 and to confirm by noninvasive underground testing the selected site of Chinggis Qa'an's tomb. Based on seven years of research, two prior visits to the location, visits to all the claimed tomb sites in Mongolia (except Altai mount site), we established the criteria for locating the Tomb of C.Q..

The expedition concluded that the selected site satisfied these criteria and completed a walking survey and magnetometric survey of the southeast plateau of the sacred mountain "housing" the tomb. According to tradition and the topography, this part of the mountain is the most logical place on the mountain to construct a tomb. Underground anomalies were discovered in the selected area but the nature of the buried material cannot be finally established until the Stanford team can fully analyze the data obtained. Further testing will probably be required. With present available equipment no final determination can be scientifically confirmed without excavation of the site.

Expedition Progress

The expedition began with a flag ceremony at the Capitol Club in Beijing (a reciprocal club with EC) organized by Steven Schwankert, the Chapter Chair of the Asia Chapter at a special first meeting of the Chapter with astronaut Member Leroy Chao making the presentation.

Afterwards the Expedition drove to the capitol of Inner Mongolia, Hohhot, for interviews and to obtain the technical equipment for underground testing which had, thankfully, been arranged by Stanford so as to avoid the strict, expensive, often unsuccessful attempts to obtain import and export licenses and even theft or damage from China customs.

This was followed by several days on the site, with most of the expedition except Nichols, commuting from nearby Bateau. The site lines were laid and surveyed by magnetometry and physical observations completed except for the north and west sides.

The expedition then traced the progress of C.Q. during his last days: the Gobi and dessert outside Zhongwei where he split his army to protect his flank from Chineese attack and launched his campaign to eliminate the Tanguts and the Xia Xia Kingdom; Yinchuan, the capital of the Xia Xia kingdom where his army finally defeated the Tanguts and now the capitol of Ningxia; south of the capital where he fell off his horse (exact place unknown); the Liu Pan mountain range, now a national park and where C.Q. died; north and west towards Mongolia along the presumed and logical route of his funeral cortege including the "Mausoleum" once claimed to be the Tomb site; across the Yellow River at the most appropriate place (geologically, directionally, and practically), and back to the site.

It was my intent with Damien LeLoup to return to the site for three days to do shallower tests along the magnetometer site lines by metal detector to determine if there was any inconsistency with the magnetometer data and to check the unlikely possibility of any caves or other sites on the west and north sides of the mountain. But that proved impossible because we had to "rescue" the rest of the field team whose vehicle was badly damaged on their early return to Beijing (no one hurt).

We were accompanied for ten days by the Conde Nast/Land Rover team who produced many hours of video and sound footage. They promised to provide the raw footage to the expedition and have done so and that has been used by Bronx TV for a pilot Explorers series and production; the expedition provided its still photographs to the Code Nast team for their use. In recognition of the services of the expedition Conde Nast/Land Rover contributed money to the Lowell Thomas dinner, hired the Club for a special event, and helped the Club explore with Land Rover possible Club sponsorship. Conde Nast published pictures and text relating to the expedition in its Traveler magazine.

Findings

I. THE SELECTED SITE SATISFIES THE REQUIRED CRITERIA.

    A. A place must be so disguised that no one has found it for over 800 years.

    B. The burial grounds and contents must be consistent with the Shaman practices and beliefs that C.Q. and his family followed: the evil spirits occupy corpses and thus require prompt burial; the Tomb must contain the implements necessary to carry out the deceased's lifetime mission in his afterlife (in C.Q.'s case to protect Mongolia and bring the whole world including southern China under his sword).

    C. There must be some evidence of a specific effort by C.Q. and his family successors to deceive anyone seeking to locate the Tomb (C.Q.'s master strategies always involved significant deception in his military tactics and strategies). See The Secret History of the Mongols and references to the guardian tribe (Kahn, Paul 2005)

    D. The burial must be on a Sacred mountain in Mongolia (at the time of his death) most likely on the southeast portion of that mountain.

    E. Obviously C.Q. is not buried in places already extensively searched in the last 750 years and particularly places searched in modem times with advanced technological equipment.

    F. Absent factual support for the location of the burial grounds, there should be some legendary support

    G. And as with any important discovery intuition should be invoked in any successful search for the Tomb.

2. WHILE MOST MONGOLIANS, AND MANY OTHERS, BELIEVE C.Q. SHOULD BE LEFT IN PEACE AND HIS OBVIOUS INTENT TO HIDE HIS TOMB SITE HONORED, THE EXPEDITION BELIEVES HIS TOMB SHOULD BE FOUND SO THAT:

    A. It can be protected, preserved, and rescued from desecration

    B. Scholars can ferret out the history of C.Q. and his times about which there is so little real historical evidence.

    C. The public can find out about the extraordinary talents and power of C.Q.

    D. Knowledge is valuable per se. Human history has always been a part of our survival and progress. The extensive artifacts with which he was buried, the recoverable DNA, and the placement of the contents and human and animal remains is a treasure of human experience and culture.

3. THE KNOWN AND INVESTIGATED ALTERNATIVE SITES DO NOT MEET REQUIRED CRITERIA ... Karakoram, the Alltai Mountains, Barkhan Khaldun, the "mausoleum", Liu Pan, numerous other suggested battlefields; forest, river, and "home" sites.

4. ONCE STANFORD HAS COMPLETED ITS ANALYSIS OF THE MAGNETOMETRY
DATA (WHICH SHOWS UNDERGROUND ANOMALIES* BUT NOT THE SPECIFIC
MATERIALS), ANOTHER VISIT WILL BE REQUIRED WITH DIFFERENT
UNDERGROUND TESTING APPARATUS AND TO ELIMINATE AS THE TOMB SITE
OTHER ADMITTEDLY UNLIKELY LOCATIONS ON THE SELECTED MOUNTAIN.
AFTERWARDS THE PROJECT MUST BE TRANSFERRED TO MORE COMPETENT
AND POWERFUL INSTITUTIONS (E.G.,GOVERNMENT AGENCIES IN CHINA,
ACADEMIC INSTITUTIONS LIKE STANFORD, UNITED NATIONS HERITAGE SITE
ORGANIZATION) ...

*Strong magnetic anomalies exist near the oval building. Further analysis may
be needed to detennine if the anomalies relate to the building foundation. The
anomalies by the cliff also may need further study and even investigation to
determine if there is a cave below (a favorite burial place for Mongol Shaman and
nobility). New measurements and a higher resolution magnetic map of the area
would be helpful for the oval building and the cliff sites.

Submitted and prepared by Alan Nichols, Leader

POEMS OF DISCOVERY...
The Secret Tomb of Chinggis Qa'an (CQ)

CLUES FOR THE CLUELESS
A clue in the 800 year search for the grave
of Chinggis Qa'an (CQ):

Here's the hint to help you find
The grave of Chinggis Qa'an
The greatest warrior of all time:

Two caskets better than one,
One silver and one wooden…
Misdirection is the key
To hide his corpse eternally.

BURY ME HERE...
There is a Mongol tradition for important leaders to pick
their own burial site.

The leader of leaders, the Qa'an of Khans,
Dies in the northern forests of Han
On the mountain range of Liu Pan.

Chinggis becomes the son of the Sun.
Who orders
"Rule for all Mongolians…

Finish your God-given tasks.
Protect your people to the last.
Conquer the world with the flash
Of your sword and your Mongol mass,
 Soldiers, loyal, strong, and fast."

CQ dies in 1227
The shaman declares
"He ascended to heaven,"
Since his casket is barren
When opened for burying.

His son put his corpse in one casket
And loaded it onto a funeral cart,
Part of the huge death dealing cortège
Of warriors, horses and sad Mongol warriors,
Swords, weapons, lances, and arrows.

When CQ's cart was stuck
In the unyielding Yellow River mud
The ghost of the Qa'an
Said, "Bury me here."
And completely in secret they did.

Everyone died who went on that ride
Or saw the Cortege coming by…
To surely conceal the corpse of the Qa'an
For all eternity from dawn to dawn
They kill all those seekers of the dead.

CQ finished his God-given tasks,
Best warrior, best Mongol Lord,
Enemies defeated, conquests succeeded,
Buried in secret to this very day
On Mountain X by the yellow bay.

DOWN...
On a Holy Mountain.

Waiting... I wait.
I wait to climb the holy Mountain...
To find a secret place that ends my wait,
A Buddha, a cave, a spiritual maze,
Alone
Anxious
Full of quit.
Nothing helps, Nothing fits...
China/America just don't mix.

Then the peak speaks to "me" — or is it "my"
Like God talks to Moses on Sinai:

> *"You should know I am it.*
> *You decide if you're in heaven*
> *Or wallowing in your own black shit."*

MONGOL LUNCH...

The Mayor of a Mongol Village (one of the few left from China's population transfer) near Mt. X invites us to lunch. We don't talk much (I don't speak Mongolian and he doesn't speak English) but toast much with "hutch," more alcohol than flower water. So we get along ideally with our friendly "hand-made" conversation.

We celebrate today
The glories of yesterday
From Chinggis Qa'an's ruling days
And his 13th century human ways.

In the Mongol shadows
From the sun and moon
From his Sky God Tenger
From our spirit's inner boons
From this holy lotus mountain —

We hear his ghostly tunes
Testament to the mightiest of men,
His power, This spirit of Chinggis Qa'an
Emperor, Shaman, Lover, Brain
Founder of China's first Yuan.

INTERVIEWS...

The True Magazine film crew videoing our expedition on the site of CQ's secret tomb interviewed me extensively many times, night and day as the Leader. It could be exhausting, time consuming, and stressful. Here's how I feel about it —

INTERVIEWS

There's nothing like our interviews
With questions wise and answers true
Building visions and egos too.

They free imagination's tools
Or prove me a poetic fool.

Interviews make me feel free,
Loved by you, or even me?
To see who am I
Or should I be.

Ask on into the night my friends...
May my postulations send
You up the river, around the bend,
To hell, then paradise in the end.

Better interviewed than cross-examined...
Better praised than denigrated...
        I still celebrate our minds' exchange
        Answering questions, good or strange.
Thanks for interviewing me today

POOR ME...

Almost angrily waiting for the driver to pass mountain X without revealing its location to a Reporter in our vehicle... A poor me attitude is a self curse and a Shugendo Jigoku experience.

I-Centered, I'm unhappy.
Anxious, I'm unfree.
Spirits,
Quell my jealousy, Eliminate "poor me"...
Don't show the holy mountain
To ruin all our plans
To save the sacred gravesite
From so many exploting hands.

I GOT THE CHINA CREDIT BLUES...

I am desperate when I realize I can't get cash with my checks or credit cards in China and all the vendors demand cash for services, equipment, hotels, food, transport etc. So I spend my first day in China going to banks, Chinese and foreign, in Beijing. It is a bank holiday in United States. But Tom from Schwab Bank arranges a temporary fix. It is touch and go for more weeks getting cash for the expedition.

5 poetically poor stanzas followed by this chorus.

CHORUS:
I got no Yuan dough
My ATM is dead
I got no way to live
No car, no food, no bed

DEAD MONEY TREE

China evaluates me
With its dead money tree.

No one accepts
My credit card reps.
Dollars dissolve into yuan/ rembi
Making life tough for the Team and me.

Without money I choke.
In effect I'm broke —
All alone on the streets of Beijing
I'm a bundle of anxious suff'ring.

Then I hear Temujin' s mother
When CQ killed his brother:
Screaming,
"You're just a dog to kill in sibling rivalry,
When, alone and lonely, we have no friends
But our shadows."

**Command rock for CQ generals directives to his
officers in Liu Pau Mountains.**

POEMS FROM
CHINGGIS QA'AN'S SPIRIT:

BOYHOOD

They claim I came from the plains
But I am from the northern woods
Swamp
Forest
River
Lake
Pond
Rain
The land of poverty.

Except for my mountain
My land is dark.
But I am the light
That will burn the world.

BOOTE*

First love and last,
I lie the world at your feet.
My honor on your breasts.
My breath in your hair.
My hand on your soul.
For ever, Boote, forever.

WARRIORS OF
THE SKY

Warriors of the Sky
Follow me
Follow me
To the horizon
Where the hills meet the clouds
Beyond our eyes.
There, glory lies
whether we live
or whether we die.
Together we'll be remembered.
We will be remembered.

* Chinggis Qa'an's wife from childhood. Although CQ had many wives, she was
ALWAYS PRIMARY, honored, respected, and powerful.

PICKING UP DAISY...

September 28, 2016 on plane returning home from Mountain X anticipating seeing our Tibetan Dharma Dog Daisy.

We are coming home Daisy
To de-kennelize your psyche.
Will you remember me?
Your 27-day absentee?
And wag your tail in ecstasy
Again to be together, buddy.
We need each other
Here and in eternity.

QUOTES FROM THE SPIRIT OF CHINGGIS QA'AN *

❖

Let's RIDE together on a road less traveled.

❖

Wrestle with men not gods.

❖

Death is anonymous.
The Sky God doesn't care what your name is.

❖

The desert will melt you into camel dung,
fuel to light The World.

❖

The river flows under the desert not on it. So should
you hide your lights, Your life saving energies.

❖

I can give you Mongolia. The rest is up to you.

❖

There is no limit on what we can rule when,
mindful and positive, we unite together.

❖

United we will rule the world forever,
Divided we will die together.

❖

Last Words of CQ…
Know a man by his weapons
His body by his teeth
His mind by his skull
His culture by his tomb
And his spirit by his horse

From the author's compendium "AlanQuotes".

Print   Close

Explorer Plans Hunt for Genghis Khan's Long-Lost Tomb

By Gene J. Koprowski

Published November 18, 2013 | FoxNews.com

The tomb of Mongolian emperor Genghis Khan -- who created the world's most powerful empire by raiding and invading across Eurasia -- is a lost treasure archaeologists have sought for years. And one man thinks he knows where it is.

Last fall Alan Nichols, the president of the Explorers Club, mapped out possible locations for the tomb of Khan (also known as Chinnggis Qa'an). His hypothesis: Khan's tomb is located in the Liupan Mountains in Northern China, where the emperor who was born in 1162 is said to have perished from an arrow wound in August 1227.

Next fall, Nichols plans the next phase of his research: pinpointing Khan's exact resting place.

"Ghengis Khan's tomb is my obsession," Nichols, a noted authority on the emperor, exclusively told FoxNews.com. "I couldn't stop thinking about it. But I'm not happy just reading about it, or knowing about it. I need to have my feet on it."

The emperor is said to be buried in a solid silver casket with amazing jewels, weapons and artifacts, as well as an entourage of warriors, slaves and horses. If successful, its discovery would be mankind's biggest archeological discovery since finding the tombs of the pharaohs in Egypt, researchers say.

"Alan has already done a great deal of the foundation work for this expedition, and while finding buried targets is always tricky and often does not succeed, Alan's plan is both timely and possible," explorer Richard Garriott, who has been on expeditions to the South Pole and the International Space Station, told FoxNews.com.

"The nomadic lifestyle of Genghis Khan and his people left a far more ethereal trace than many more settled civilizations. Finding the tomb would very likely unearth a wealth of artifacts that would tell the story of this important and powerful leader, in ways we will only speculate about otherwise," he added.

Magnetometry, underground testing

Ever since Marco Polo, explorers have been looking for the tomb of Chinnggis Qa'an, Nichols said. But new archaeology tools may help them succeed where others fail.

"Our current knowledge and tools concerning magnetometry and other underground testing techniques now available will vastly change the exploration opportunities," Nichols said.

The place of Genghis Khan's death is said by locals to be marked with a circle of stones. On Nichols' last trip, he had his team drive 1,300 miles to a remote mountain locale—seldom visited by anyone but the indigenous persons there—to retrace the path to the so-called sacred "Mountain X."

Nichols now believes the Luipan Mountains that rise above the grasslands are the final resting place of the famed emperor, a short flight north of Hong Kong, near the Yellow River, off the coast of the Pacific Ocean. The site is 5,000 feet above sea level, and houses the ruins of a Buddhist temple, where smiling Buddhist sculptures overlooking the mountain.

There, Nichols and his colleagues Warren Caldwell, a PhD candidate in geophysics at Stanford University, and explorer Mike Pizzio roamed the ancient countryside in a Land Rover LR4. There are five so-called sacred mountains in China that have been the subject of imperial pilgrimages by emperors throughout history. Khan is said by lore and word of mouth to have died at the foot of one in the Luipan Mountains.

www.foxnews.com/science/2013/11/18/explorer-plans-hunt-for-genghis-khans-long-lost-tomb/print

On his last day in the field, last fall, Nichols made a find on that mountainside: a marker with a message covered by moss. The clue was not in any of the books he's read on Khan or searchable online. This inscription brought him another step closer to fulfilling this mission, he said.

"Genghis Khan was a brutal, bloodthirsty conqueror, but his death and the legacy he established deserve a historical marker," Prof. Usha Haley, at West Virginia University, an expert on the Silk Road, and author of *The Chinese Tao of Business*, told FoxNews.com.

Ghengis Khan's grandson Kublai Khan founded a dynasty in China, so the emperor's legacy is a long-lasting one in Chinese history.

"Kublai Khan, who hosted Marco Polo, founded the Chinese Yuan dynasty which lasted for a century. Genghis Khan's legacy includes carrying cultural and artistic accomplishments through the Pax Mongolica and over the Silk Road across the largest empire ever -- from the Pacific Ocean to modern-day Hungary, including Asia.

"Maintaining this empire required imaginative leadership, administrative skills, adroit use of the military technology of the day -- along with outrageous violence and destruction."

Many expeditions have tried in the past to find the tomb of the great warrior, but all have failed or proved inconclusive, relying on guidance from the Chinese government. Nichols' and crew's next trek -- next year is the scheduled timeframe -- may change history.

"This discovery would be on the scale of the discovery in Egypt of the tombs of Pharaohs. But in this case, there is one and only one Genghis Khan, not the rich lineage of Pharaohs found in Egypt," Garriott told FoxNews.com.

Established in 1904, the Explorers Club is a professional society, like the National Geographic Society, dedicated to the advancement of field research. The club awards its distinguished "flag" to expeditions it deems important to furthering scientific knowledge in specific fields.

Print   ✕ Close

URL

http://www.foxnews.com/science/2013/11/18/explorer-plans-hunt-for-genghis-khans-long-lost-tomb/

Home | Video | Politics | U.S. | Opinion | Entertainment | Tech | Science | Health | Travel | Lifestyle | World | Sports | Weather

Privacy | Terms

This material may not be published, broadcast, rewritten, or redistributed. © 2013 FOX News Network, LLC. All rights reserved. All market data delayed 20 minutes.

NO BONE UNTURNED

POSTSCRIPT IV

Where was Genghis Khan buried? Explorer Alan Nichols says he knows the answer – and everyone else is looking in the wrong place, writes **Tessa Chan**

For nearly 800 years, archaeologists, treasure hunters, scientists, explorers and more have been searching for the tomb of 13th century Mongolian emperor Genghis Khan. Many have dedicated their lives to the search. And yet, no one has found him.

The problem is they're all looking in the wrong place, according to 86-year-old American explorer, author and lawyer Alan Nichols.

The former president of the New York-based Explorers Club, Nichols, who led nine of its flag expeditions, is an expert in sacred mountains and was the first person to cycle the entire Silk Road from Turkey to China.

Most previous efforts to find the resting place of the founder of the Mongol empire have concentrated around Burkhan Khaldun, a sacred mountain in the Khentii province of northeastern Mongolia. The mountain was believed to be near Genghis Khan's birthplace, and a special spiritual refuge for him.

"That's where all the modern guys are," says Nichols. "[National Geographic adventurer] Albert Lin is up there, [archaeologist Maury] Kravitz was there, the Japanese and a whole bunch of smaller searches. They're all wrong."

Nichols is confident he has nailed down the location of the burial site, which he refers to as "Mountain X" for reasons of confidentiality. "For now, all I can say is that it's somewhere within the historical Mongol empire, though the borders of China and Mongolia in those days were non-existent, since he had conquered northern China," he says. The search has been gaining momentum, thanks to ever more accessible air travel and new technology. Lin, a research scientist at University of

California, San Diego has been leading an international crowdsourcing effort to search for the tomb using non-invasive technology such as satellite-based remote sensing, asking people around the world to tag anomalies on images taken from space, which could indicate man-made structures underground.

"That's big money and big manpower," says Nichols. "Albert Lin, he's a great guy, he has a lab [that's] darn near half a block. It's one huge lab with maybe 10 or 12 graduate students – and he is developing drones, satellite imagery, caves and all this wonderful stuff.

"So I love to tell him, God that's the most impressive stuff I've ever seen. The only problem is, you're a thousand miles away."

When we speak via video conference, Nichols is about to set off on a flag-bearing expedition to locate the tomb, bringing with him a team of experts and the latest underground testing equipment to prove it.

He has been researching and preparing for this trip for 10 years, and his theory is based on a set of criteria he has developed for locating the site.

One of the main reasons he's convinced the burial site is not in the Khentii Mountains is that the Great Khan – who, he claims, was actually called Chinggis Qa'an – was a master of deception.

Whether measured by the number of people defeated, countries annexed or total area occupied, Khan conquered more than twice as much as any other man in history, according to Jack Weatherford, author of *Genghis Khan and the Making of the Modern World* (2004). One of his most successful war

Granite rock formations of the Khentii Mountains in Mongolia, where most of the searches have been focused. Nichols is looking elsewhere.

strategies was the "Dog Fight", whereby his armies would fool his enemies into thinking they were retreating, lure them away from their villages, then surprise them with an attack when they were tired, weak and dispersed.

"He was a genius at deception; you don't think he's going to use it? And being as wonderful as he is, he's managed to deceive all these fabulously smart people – including Marco Polo."

Many differing legends surround the burial of Khan, who died in 1227, in Western Xia (in today's northwestern China) in his mid-60s. There are different stories about how he died; some say he was killed in action, others suspect it was from a wound, and one rumour spread by his detractors even suggested that a captured Tangut queen inserted a contraption into her vagina that ripped his sexual organs, causing him to bleed to death.

According to popular belief, a cortege of soldiers escorted the body back to Mongolia for a secret burial, killing every person and animal they met along the way. Eight hundred horsemen

> **Genghis Khan was a genius at deception ... he's managed to deceive all these fabulously smart people – including Marco Polo**
>
> ALAN NICHOLS (LEFT), AMERICAN EXPLORER, AUTHOR AND LAWYER

An illustration of Genghis Khan leading the Mongol conquests.

then trampled the area to obscure its location, and then they too were killed so they couldn't reveal the grave's location, as were the soldiers who killed them – and the soldiers who killed them.

"It's not possible that it's in the Khentii because Chinggis Qa'an and his family made a big deal out of taking a casket up there," says Nichols. "It's the first place everybody would think of."

The Mongols believe a body should not be disturbed. Every warrior had a Spirit Banner, which was constructed by tying strands of hair from a warrior's best stallions to his spear, and that's where the spirit went when they died. "Dying? That's something the Mongolians didn't even think about. You transisted; you changed states."

Many people have claimed to know the location of Genghis Khan's tomb, but none have been able to prove it. One website reported a couple of years ago that construction workers in Khentii had stumbled upon the royal burial site. However, another article says they've found proof that Jesus was an alcoholic.

Nichols is well aware that the Mongolians want the body to be left in peace. He says his fellow researchers there have told him they hope he doesn't find it; they don't want anybody to find it, let alone a foreigner.

"So, why would we look for him? We know Chinggis Qa'an didn't want it, and I have absolute respect for him," says Nichols. "The answer is this: I have a list, and there's at least 70 separate important things on that list that I can find about Genghis Khan and his people from what I know is in his tomb. I can tell you about his religion, his clothes, his nutrition, his war strategy, and of course race – where the Mongols came from. So it gives you unbelievable information."

The second reason, he adds, is that if he doesn't find him, somebody else will, and part of his objective is to protect and conserve the site.

"The fact is, everybody who's looking for him has got some axe to grind: you want to find him to get all the glory. Because you want the gold and silver. Or because you're a professor and you want to be a big hero in the academic world."

Nichols has been to the site three times and has already detected anomalies. This time he's returning armed with the latest non-invasive equipment: an advanced form of magnetometry and ground piercing radars. Among the proof he's looking for are a silver casket, horses, bones, gold and silver, weapons and siege machinery.

"Let's say I'm wrong. Let's say I get under there and I find sheep bones. But – and this is true of all science – the guy who finds the cure for cancer, or immunisation for this or that, he's dependent on all the other brilliant guys who tried something else and were wrong. I don't have to bother with Burkhan Khaldun, because Lin's up there, and he's as sophisticated as you can get.

"And will I take a chance? I'm not insane – it could be a failure, you always have to face that chance. But if I don't find it, hopefully somebody is going to in my lifetime. Or maybe not. This Chinggis Qa'an was a really creative guy."

tessa.chan@scmp.com

To be continued: the *South China Morning Post* will be following Alan Nichols' expedition closely, and providing updates on his progress

Tessa Chan
(tessa.chan@scmp.com)
from the
SOUTH CHINA MORNING POST MAGAZINE
November 20, 2016

https://multimedia.scmp.com/magazines/post-magazine/article/genghis-khan/index.html

Looking for Chinggis

The location of Genghis Khan's burial site is an 800-year-old mystery that has captured the imagination of explorers and scholars alike. American adventurer Alan Nichols believes he may be one step closer to solving the puzzle.

WORDS AND PICTURES **TESSA CHAN**

"I COULD TELL YOU where Genghis Khan is buried," says Alan Nichols, the first time we speak, "But then I'd have to shoot you."

We laugh, but I am not sure the American explorer isn't serious; after all, it's a mystery that's endured for nearly 800 years.

There have been many attempts to find Genghis' tomb by grave robbers, adventurers and archaeologists. Most have been centred on Burkhan Khaldun, in the Kheutii province of northeastern Mongolia, the great warrior's birthplace. According to *The Secret History of the Mongols* (1240), the oldest surviving literary work on the last days of Genghis, he sought refuge here, worshipped here, declared it the most sacred mountain in Mongolia and - most intriguingly - exclaimed, "Bury me here when I pass away." However, all searches of the area have proved fruitless.

After a decade of research, Nichols, 86, an attorney, published author and expert on Tibet and China, is convinced Genghis' final resting place is elsewhere. He invited me to join an expedition to show the tomb is hidden where he thinks it is, but his emails were so cryptic that only at the last minute did I know which country to book flights to.

At first, all I was told was that we were going "somewhere in historical Mongolia"; the route and plans changing in the days leading up to our meeting.

His obsession with secrecy is largely due to concerns about what could happen should knowledge of the burial site fall into the wrong hands. Not only would the discovery of the tomb of the founder of the Mongol empire be of huge historical significance, it's also believed to be full of jewellery, precious metals and relics.

"I'm very careful about not telling people where it is," he says. "I have agreements with all the technical people - I'm a lawyer, as you know - and I've already thought how to make sure that nobody lets it out" before, that is, he's been able to go through the correct channels and guarantee some measure of protection.

NICHOLS WAS THE 42nd president of the Explorers Club, a New York-founded international society that promotes scientific exploration, and he holds several world firsts, including being the first Westerner to circumambulate Tibet's most sacred mountain, Mount Kailas, and the first to cycle the entire Silk Road. He's been studying sacred mountains for 60 years but Nichols' search for Genghis' tomb is contentious.

"Mongolians are fairly unanimous in not wanting their founder to be disturbed," says Mongolia-based American professor and anthropologist Jack Weatherford, author of *Genghis Khan and the Making of the Modern World* (2004). "He said, 'Let my body die, but let my nation live.' Therefore, people should ignore the body and concentrate on the welfare of the nation. The idea that anyone would search for the tomb is disturbing for most Mongols, and the idea of foreigners searching for it can be quite alarming."

Genghis was a master of deception. He would mislead enemies into thinking his men were retreating when they were lying in wait and use propaganda to spread fear about the size and ferocity of his army. Although most historians agree he was killed on August 18, 1227, during the fall of Yinchuan, there is surprisingly little in writing about how the warrior died or his burial.

"Mongols have strict taboos about discussing death, so very little is recorded," says Weatherford. "This created many opportunities for foreigners to write all types of imaginative and speculative scenarios of what happened."

Some say he was struck by lightning, others that he was killed by a vengeful queen, while still others believe he was killed in battle or falling off his horse.

He *is* said, however, to have left clear instructions that nobody should disturb his remains. One legend has it that the 1,000 soldiers who carried the khan's body to its burial site were killed to prevent them from disclosing its location, then those who killed the burial brigade were also dispatched, and thousands of horses were released to trample the ground in which he was buried, to hide any trace of it as having been disturbed. Other stories tell of a forest being planted or a river diverted, to hide the site.

There was excitement when Genghis' palace was discovered by a Japanese-Mongolian expedition in 2004, as ancient texts refer to officials travelling daily between the palace grounds and the burial site, to conduct rituals, yet the tomb was not found.

One of the most dedicated Genghis hunters, American amateur archaeologist Maury Kravitz, spent 40 years searching for the tomb near Burkhan Khaldun, and reportedly had to pull out of one excavation due to a series of unfortunate events that included team members being bitten by pit vipers and cars rolling off hills for no apparent reason - reinforcing beliefs that the tomb is protected by a curse. That expedition was publicly condemned by a former

Mongolian prime minister but Kravitz continued his efforts until he died of heart disease, aged 80, in 2012.

Hope has been revived in recent years by technological advances. California-based research scientist Albert Lin Yu-Min has been leading a crowdsourcing effort to analyse satellite imagery and employ non-invasive tools to search for anomalies underground near Burkhan Khaldun.

Convinced everyone else is hundreds of miles off the mark, however, Nichols has zeroed in on a sacred site he refers to simply as "Mountain X", and is now attempting to prove that this is where Genghis' remains lie.

"I already know that there are anomalies down there," he says. "I know something is under that ground that is not part of the ground."

What makes him so sure?

"I've already been on three expeditions, and I spent the first seven years developing criteria [including distance, terrain and allowances for shamanistic beliefs and the probable use of deception] for locating the tomb of Chinggis Qa'an", which, according to Nichols, is a more accurate rendering of the name.

A FEW WEEKS AFTER our initial phone call, I meet Nichols and his crew over breakfast in Yinchuan, now the capital of the Ningxia Hui autonomous region. They've been in the field for two weeks and have been taking readings on Mountain X using magnetometers and a ground-penetrating radar.

Pocketing a USB stick full of data they'll spend the next few months analysing, Nichols introduces me to the team. For the final leg of his expedition, I am joining magnetometer expert Jerry Griffith, doctor Stew Lauterbach ("Who's here to keep me alive," says Nichols), the explorer's wife, Becky, a documentary film crew, drivers Qiang and Hao Lipeng and translator Zhu Yvette Youjia, who is also in charge of logistics.

"Our selected site is somewhat complicated, because right now it's a construction zone," says Griffith, without giving me the slightest idea of how far we are from Mountain X. "So we're trying to take the readings around heavy equipment and construction workers. But we took 48 plots or grids and, hopefully, we have enough data to piece together what we want to know, which is whether Genghis Khan's tomb is where we think it is."

Our objective over the next week will be to trace the route Genghis' funeral cortege would have followed.

Explorer Alan Nichols in the Tengger Desert, in Inner Mongolia, in September.

89

"We know that he had to be taken from where he died, in [Ningxia's] Liupan Mountains, back to ancient Mongolia," says Nichols. "He's a Mongolian leader and there's no way you'd bury him in China. So the point now is to track how he got there – nobody's actually established that before."

We have to prove that it's not only a feasible route, but a fast one, he adds.

"According to Mongolian shamanism, which governs all of this, he must be buried promptly, because when a person dies his spirit goes into his spirit banner, but his bones are invaded by evil forces. You can't even touch a corpse without dangerous consequences to yourself: physical, mental and emotional."

While on the road, I receive an email from Hong Kong-based Swiss adventurer and Mongolia expert Marc Progin, who read my first article, announcing the expedition. Questioning Nichols' motives, Progin urges him to respect the wishes of the Mongolians and call off the search.

"I'd say to those who don't want him to be found, 'He's going to be found,'" says Nichols, when I mention the message. "He's the most famous warrior in the history of the world.

"We now have satellite imagery, drones, ground-penetrating radar. We have all sorts of things, both from military and from mineral research. They're going to find it, and they're going to find it soon. And if it's not found by someone who wants to take it to the next step – which is to find the right institutions and way to protect those remains – it'll be another Disneyland."

Is it the glory he's after? After all, what explorer wouldn't want to be remembered as the man who solved one of history's greatest mysteries?

Nichols says it's neither the glory nor the gold he's seeking.

"Education in Europe and the US is appallingly poor as to Genghis Khan," he says, citing freedom of religion and diplomacy as just some of the ideas the famous conqueror introduced. "I mean, we talk about Caesar, Alexander ... they're nothing compared with Chinggis Qa'an in what they accomplished. So I think that the idea of preserving this memory and this knowledge is important."

We spend the first few days driving along backroads, studying terrain, looking for places that would be impassable for a horse- or oxen-drawn cart carrying a corpse.

Over the week, Nichols narrows down his hypothetical route by a process of elimination. We follow a railway line that heads north to Zhongwei.

"Railways have to be basically flat," says Nichols. "Of course, there were no railroads in 1227, but that's a huge hint. This railroad gives us the track from the Liupan Mountains: flat and straight through this valley to the Yellow River."

On day four, we pull up in a jeep at the surreal Shapotou Tourist Zone, with its enormous castle entrance, coloured flags flapping in the wind, pop music blaring from loud-speakers and golf carts taking tourists out to embark on overpriced camel tours. Nichols explains to the perplexed cameleers that we aren't interested in taking the tourist route and want to ride their beasts north instead. He wants to test how far a camel can travel across desert sands in a day.

"I can't talk about how long it takes a camel to go up this desert to Mongolia unless I've done it myself," he says. "I've always found that it's vitally important to be hands-on."

From left: Nichols and his camel, Homer, in Shapotou; the explorer studies a map on his way out of Yinchuan.

"They're going to find it, and they're going to find it soon. And if it's not found by someone who wants to take it to the next step – which is to find the right institutions and way to protect those remains – it'll be another Disneyland"

Says Lauterbach, "Alan does his exploring in a shoe-leather fashion, where you go out and really beat the pavement to find the information. And he's doing it in the classic old-fashioned way. It's fascinating to watch him work."

We become hypnotised by the alien landscape of the Tengger Desert and the lurching movements of the camels. Our ride resembles little what a Mongol army's would have been like, but gives an idea of how time-consuming it is to cross such challenging terrain. The dunes are steep and the sand gives way under the camels' feet, causing them to slide and stumble; the fact that they're tied together on a short rope doesn't help.

We set up camp just before nightfall and, watching him walk up the dunes, his feet sinking into the sand, for the first time I worry that Nichols looks tired. It's easy to forget his age because we spend most of the time struggling to keep up with him.

"He's driven," observes Griffith. "And he pushes himself – physically, spiritually and intellectually."

"Alan really is formidable," says Hao, who is also a chef and hotelier. "The way he climbs mountains and things – you wouldn't see Chinese men of his age doing this."

For his part, Nichols, whose motto is that anything can be done at any age (it just takes a little longer), says he feels exhilarated.

"I have given up my hypothesis of the cortege going north through here," he says. "You'd never take a cart, even if it was pulled by camels, through this. This would be a really big job even for Chinggis Qa'an, with his unlimited camels, troops, resources."

The procession would have travelled along the outskirts of the desert, he suggests. Most experts believe the funeral cart was drawn by oxen, but "I asked the cameleers here, what about oxen?" says Nichols. "The oxen are too low, they wouldn't go through the sand. A camel can go a week without water or food.

"Ours were very slow-paced camels. But just camels like

this – and he would have had warrior camels – can travel 60km to 80km a day. Add to that the fact that Mongol warriors would be moving day and night."

That night we eat by a fire, Nichols serenading us with 1930s campfire songs while the cameleers teach the film crew raucous drinking games.

In the morning, the sand is smooth except for snake trails and the footprints left by lizards and small mammals. While we ride, a large grey fox sprints away from us across the dunes.

Leaving the desert the next day, we detour to the swampy banks of the Yellow River, in Yinchuan, before heading out on a long, dusty drive towards Ordos, in Inner Mongolia.

"WE'RE STANDING ON A battlefield," says Nichols, pacing the muddy ground. "We're at a place that was critical to Chinggis Qa'an's attack on the Tanguts," he says, referring to the 1226 Battle of the Yellow River, part of Genghis' campaign to conquer the Western Xia empire.

"The best defence from Mongol cavalry? Water. So the Tanguts built ditches, lakes ... but Chinggis waited till wintertime, when it froze."

Mongol horses could swim but a funeral procession would have had to transport heavy carts across the river, he says. "And they did that, but they wouldn't walk along the river like we are and get bogged down."

As we drive out of Ningxia – home to Hui Muslims – to Ordos, the script on the road signs changes from the horizontal Arabic to the vertical Mongolian, even though Mongolians make up just 20 per cent of the population in Inner Mongolia.

We take six-lane highways past colossal skyscrapers, many of them ghostly empty shells, lit up at night only by the neon lights lining their exterior.

Our route changes as

Translator Yvette Zhu (left) and magnetometer expert Jerry Griffith look out over the Liupan Mountains, where Genghis Khan is believed to have died.

The Mausoleum of Genghis Khan, in Ordos, Inner Mongolia.

Nichols updates his hypothesis according to his findings. He scribbles in a small notebook he keeps in his pocket and quizzes locals – tour guides, drivers and professors – for information, all the time being careful not to reveal his mission.

Our final stop is the Mausoleum of Genghis Khan, in Ordos, an area the warrior was believed to have admired in 1227. It holds artefacts, including his saddle and bow, and inside there are statues of Genghis, incense, signs urging visitors to make donations and souvenir shops selling trinkets featuring his face. Despite the name, few believe Genghis' body is buried in this "mausoleum", which was built in 1954 by a Chinese government keen to adopt the legendary warrior as a national hero.

LATER, WHEN I TELL Weatherford I'm struggling to find a Mongolian expert willing to share their point of view for this story, he explains that, language barriers aside, such issues are politically sensitive.

"Scholars in many countries have claimed that the site is in their country – Mongolia, China, Russia and Kazakhstan, in particular," says the anthropologist. "The claim of finding a tomb in any one of these countries would be somewhat alarming to the others and might be interpreted as a claim that that country is heir to the world empire of Genghis Khan."

Eventually, Naran Bilik, a distinguished Inner Mongolian professor specialising in anthropology and ethnicity at Fudan University, Shanghai, replies somewhat cryptically to my emails. He says efforts to discover Genghis' body have to take into account at least three factors.

"First, the subjectivity of the locals is vital since Genghis Khan means a lot to them," he says. "Second, even amongst the Mongols there are different sections and private individuals – who can represent the Mongols? Are Inner Mongolians part of those who have a voice in such matters? Thirdly, it is a matter of negotiation and compromise, eventually. All parties involved have a stake in it and they have to strike a balance between different claims."

Nichols says he's aware of the sensitivities.

"I feel that responsibility to do my best. In fact, I even thought at one time that if I was unable to get the right people involved, I would not tell anybody. Or, like Chinggis Qa'an would do: I would tell them the wrong place," he says. "I have an obligation to protect the tomb. And I'm not big enough to do it myself. It'd have to be the United Nations; it has to be cooperative. And the world has to know about it, and expect that we're going to preserve this memory."

Nichols says he thinks the analysis of the data he and his team have collected will be complete by March.

"As a scholar I look forward to learning about what he finds," says Weatherford. "Yet, as a person who loves Mongolia deeply, I also love the mystery surrounding the end of Genghis Khan's life."

And if you're thinking this is the explorer's last big shot at glory before he retires, you're mistaken.

"This is definitely not my last expedition," says Nichols.

His next? All I can say is that it will take him into remotest Bhutan.

I could tell you more, but then I'd have to shoot you. ∎

Alan Nichols' route, decided through on-the-ground research and a process of elimination, shows the funeral cortege following what is now a railway line through a valley from the Liupan Mountains, skirting the Tengger Desert and heading towards "Mountain X".

Nichols' map

What might be found in the tomb?

Nichols joins a tai chi session in Liupanshan town ... at the entraqnce of today's Liupanshan park (where CQ died).

The expedition team test how far a camel can travel across dunes in a day, followed by film-makers Caleb Seppala and Jackson McCoy;

Rigorous research and a difficult drive through harsh terrain lead the hunter to a former battle-field by the banks of the Yellow River. The area was critical to Chinggis Qa'an's attack on the Tanguts in 1226, a year before he died.

Liupanshan, like most of the towns in the area, is experiencing a lot ofconstuction, though many of the buildings remain empty.

Chinggis Qa'an's invasion route against the Tanguts but not the cortege route to his grave.

The World Daily News Report on June 18, 2016 reported on the internet that "Archaeologists Unearthed the Tomb of Genghis Khan".

According to the World Daily News Story on the internet: "Road builders in Northern Mongolia near the Onon River in Khenti providence during highway construction unearthed a tomb with weapons, jewels, gold, silver and many human and horse bones.

Archeologists concluded this was the actual tomb of Chinggis Qa'an never found before after over a 750 year search.

 NEW CARS CURIOSITY SCIENCE USEFUL FUTURE TECHN

OTHER STORIES THAT HAVE APPEARED IN THE WORLD DAILY NEWS

http://worldnewsdailyreport.com/

`Science`

MONGOLIA: ARCHAEOLOGISTS UNEARTH TOMB OF GENGHIS KHAN

📅 December 10, 2016 👤 bimba 1 Comment

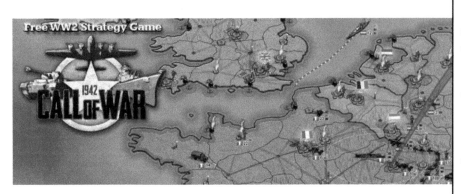

Construction workers employed in road building near the Onon River in the Khentii province of Mongolia, have discovered a mass grave containing the remains of many dozens of human corpses lying upon a large rudimentary stone structure. Forensic experts and archaeologists were called on the site, which was revealed to be a Mongolian royal tomb from the 13th century that the scientists believe to be Genghis Khan's.

The team of scientists affiliated with the University of Beijing, has

OTHER STORIES THAT HAVE APPEARED IN THE WORLD DAILY NEWS

"Foster Parents Forced Children to Eat Dog"

"Qatar: Man Arrested for Smuggling Bacon In His Anal Cavity"

" Moon: Soviet Flag Spotted on Moon Sparks Debate About Secret Moon Landing"

"Canada: Man Born with Micropenis Is Denied Legally Assisted Suicide"

"Israel: Newly Found Second Century Scroll Claims Jesus Was An Alcoholic"

"Pacific: Jap Whaling Crew Eaten Alive by Killer Whales, 16 Dead"

"Germany: German Scientists Prove There Is Life After Death"

Australia: 600 Pound Woman Gives Birth To 40 Pound Baby"

"Yoko Ono: I Had An Affair with Hilary Clinton"

"Washington, D.C.: Hilary Clinton Promises To Obey the Law And Never Lie Again."

New York City, Trump Tower: Trump appoints Chinggis Qa'an spirit advisor to his War Cabinet"

concluded that the numerous skeletons buried on top of the structure were most likely the slaves who built it and who were then massacred to keep the secret of the location. The remains of twelve horses were also found on the site, certainly sacrificed to accompany the Great Khan in death.

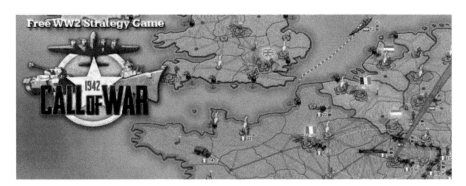

A total of 68 skeletons were found buried together, almost directly over the top of a rather crude stone structure.

The content of the tomb was scattered and badly deteriorated, presumably due to the fact that the site was located beneath the river bed for hundreds of years, until the course of the Onon river changed in the 18th century. The remains of a tall male and sixteen female skeletons were identified among hundreds of gold and silver artefacts and thousands of coins. The women are presumed to have been wives and concubines of the leader, who were killed to accompany the warlord in the afterlife.

The amount of treasure and the number of sacrificed animals and people, have immediately led the archaeologists to consider that the site was certainly the burial site of a really powerful Mongol warlord. After realizing an extensive set of tests and analysis, they were able to confirm that the body belonged to a man aged between 60 and 75, who died between 1215 and 1235 AD. Both the age, the date, the location and the opulence of the site seem to confirm that the tomb does indeed belong to Genghis Khan.

The simple rock dome discovered by the archaeologists, was presumably buried beneath the Onon river for centuries.

The incontestable historical importance of Genghis Khan makes this new discovery one of the most important in the history of archaeology. Born Temüjin (which means "of iron"), he was the founder and Great Khan (emperor) of the Mongol Empire, which became the largest contiguous empire in history after his demise. He is known for uniting the warring tribes of Mongolia and merging them into one before launching a series of military campaigns in China, Central Asia, the Middle East and even Eastern Europe. He conquered more than 31 million square kilometers of land during his lifetime.

His legacy has taken many forms besides his conquest and can still be found today, making him one of the most influential men in the history of mankind. He connected the East and the West through the creation of the Silk Route, a trade route that would become and remain for centuries, the main network of trade and cultural transmission in Eurasia, opening long-distance, political and economic interactions between the civilizations.

Genghis Khan also has an incredible number of descendants, as some genetic studies have shown that he could be the direct ancestor of 1 human out every 200 who are alive today. In Mongolia alone as many as 200,000 of the country's 2 million people could be Genghis Khan descendants.

http://worldnewsdailyreport.com/

Condé Nast
Traveler

TRUTH IN TRAVEL

JANUARY 2013

ROMAN HOLIDAY The good life
on a terrace of the Villa Cupola suite
at the Westin Excelsior, Rome.

$4.99US $5.99FOR

08434   0 757358 3

01>

SEEKING GENGHIS KHAN'S GREAT SECRET

AN ADVENTURE THROUGH INNER MONGOLIA

FOR MORE THAN 750 YEARS, the exact location of Genghiṣ Khan's burial has remained a mystery.

While scholars speculate and historians ponder, one lifelong adventurer took the matter into his own hands. This past September, Dr. Alan Nichols loaded up a Land Rover LR4 and spent two weeks trekking through the remote regions and burgeoning cities of China to retrace the last days of Genghis Khan (known by the more accurate transliteration of Chinggis Qa'an among the expedition team). Alan's quest was personal. Through years of research and something called faith, he zeroed in on a sacred mountain rising over vast grasslands and potentially holding the secrets of history's greatest empire. With this singular vision, his adventure to find the lost tomb began.

PRESENTED BY **LAND ROVER**

ABOVE AND BEYOND

94

BEIJING

A JOURNEY ACROSS TIME AND TERRAIN

HIGHLIGHTS FROM THE EXPEDITION REVEAL THE TRIUMPHS OF THE JOURNEY—FROM THE FIRST SMALL STEPS TOWARD PROVING HIS HYPOTHESIS TO UNEXPECTED FINDS ALONG THE WAY.

MONGOLIA

Inner Mongolia

Hebei

Hohhot & Baotou
②
① Beijing

The Grasslands
③

Liupan Mountains
④

Ordos Desert
⑤

Ningxia

Yinchuan

YELLOW SEA

YELLOW RIVER

Xi'an

CHINA

Chengdu

MOUNTAIN X

Hong Kong

Macau

PACIFIC OCEAN

500 km
500 mi

YINCHUAN

RETRACING THE FINAL DAYS OF GENGHIS KHAN
MEANS CONFRONTING CHALLENGING CONDITIONS AT EVERY TURN

THE EXPEDITION ROUTE took Alan and his team from the frenzied streets of Beijing to the jagged roads of China's coal corridor, through rivers, deserts, and grasslands, and over steep mountain passages. The final stop: a sumptuous hotel where they could recover from weeks of dust and deprivation.

With a V-8 engine, four-corner electronic air suspension, and Terrain Response with five settings—from general driving to rock crawl—the LR4 carried them in comfort and confidence from hopeful beginning to luxuriant end.

① BEIJING

Objective: China's capital is a city of more than twenty million. As the start and end point of the expedition, it had all the material comforts and modern resources the team needed, but traffic and sudden obstructions are a constant.

Capabilities: **Stopping power is a hallmark of the LR4. An all-terrain* anti-lock brake system* caters to the LR4's enhanced performance and improves braking feel.**

② HOHHOT & BAOTOU

Objective: Between these two fast-growing cities stands the proposed site of Genghis Khan's tomb. The expedition team spent days in the region conducting enthnographic and geophysical research amid flooded, roads and the Yellow River's tributaries.

Capabilities: **The LR4 maximum wading depth with air suspension raised is 27.56 inches.**

*These systems are not a substitute for driving safely with due care and attention and will not feature under all circumstances, speeds, weather and road conditions, etc. Driver should not assume that these systems will correct errors of judgment in driving. Please consult the owner's manual or your local authorized Land Rover Retailer for more details.

Alan developed nine conditions for identifying the site of Genghis Khan's tomb. One sacred mountain near the Yellow River in Inner Mongolia—the highest peak shown here—met all his criteria. The expedition team named it Mountain X.

John Rice

"Genghis Khan's tomb became my obsession—I couldn't stop thinking about it. But I'm not happy just reading about it or knowing about it. I need to have my feet on it."

–Alan Nichols, Expedition Leader

Hiroshi Hara/A Famdy Affair Films

Hiroshi Hara/A Family Affair Films

Warren Caldwell

❸ THE GRASSLANDS

Objective: To fully understand the skills demanded of Genghis Khan's massive armies of horsemen, the expedition team crossed the same terrain they once conquered. Here, high grasses and extreme temperatures determined a way of life.

Capabilities: With four-corner air suspension, the LR4 can raise the ride height up to 4.92 inches for off-road use, optimizing vehicle setup for different terrain conditions and inspiring confidence over mud, gravel, grass, snow, and rocks.

❹ LIUPAN MOUNTAINS

Objective: The place of Genghis Khan's death is marked with a circle of stones. The team drove 1,300 miles to this remote mountain locale—seldom visited by anyone but locals—to retrace the path from here to Mountain X.

Capabilities: In the LR4, Hill Descent Control (HDC)* with Gradient Release Control (GRC)* comes standard. This system allows a smooth, controlled descent without the need to use the brake or accelerator. GRC provides more gradual acceleration on a steep incline.

❺ YINCHUAN & THE ORDOS DESERT

Objective: Yinchuan is a booming city surrounded by a vast desert laced with unpaved roads. Here, the team gathered oral histories and enlisted camels to re-create the movements of the historic funeral cortege.

Capabilities: The LR4 features an expanded Terrain Response® system* optimizing the vehicle setup for virtually all on-road or off-road driving situations. Its Sand Launch Control (SLC)* setting helps prevent wheel spin and the vehicle "digging in" when moving from a standstill.

96

ADVERTISEMENT

Founded in 1904, the Explorers Club is a professional society dedicated to the advancement of field research. The club awards flags to expeditions it deems important to furthering knowledge in specific fields.

While chaos surrounded them outside—mile after mile of unpaved roads, air thick with dust and grime, traffic jams of lumbering coal trucks, rogue bicycles, rattling carts, and even a few flocks of sheep—the expedition team found an oasis of calm within.

THE WINDING ROAD TO DISCOVERY

IN EVERY EXPEDITION, THE UNEXPECTED MUST BE EXPECTED.
EACH TURN ON ALAN'S JOURNEY OFFERED A NEW CHALLENGE, A NEW REVELATION.

THE EXPEDITION TEAM

DR. ALAN NICHOLS

Dr. Alan Nichols has led and participated in expeditions in the U.S., China, Japan, India, Bhutan, Nepal, Europe, South America, and Africa. He is the author of several books, including *To Climb a Sacred Mountain*, and is the president of the Explorers Club.

WARREN CALDWELL

Warren Caldwell is a Ph.D. candidate in geophysics at Stanford University. His research applies earthquake seismology to study the tectonic collision of India and Asia.

MIKE PIZZIO

Mike Pizzio's personal and professional experiences have placed him in extreme conditions ranging from mixed-gas deep dives to crime scene investigations. He is a member of the Explorers Club.

❶ FIRST STEPS ON MOUNTAIN X

To the expedition team it is Mountain X: the proposed site of Genghis Khan's tomb. By night the team camped in a temple under the protection of a smiling Buddha, by day they conducted geophysical research. To mark this critical first step in testing the expedition's hypothesis, Alan and Mike made a symbolic journey 5,000 feet above sea level to the mountain's peak.

97

ADVERTISEMENT

❸ CONFRONTING THE YELLOW RIVER

The Yellow River winds a storied path through China, once providing a natural border in the expanding empire of Genghis Khan. Far too wide and foreboding to cross in most sections, its tributaries posed no barrier for the LR4.

❷ INSIDE A MONGOL VILLAGE

Ethnographic research was key to the expedition. A meeting with a local elder, held deep in the maze of a Mongol village, yielded a precious gift: a photo of a temple destroyed by fire in the 1960s—a vital link in Alan's path backward in time.

❹ A PILGRIMAGE TO THE TANGUT KINGDOM

The final conquest of Genghis Khan was the Tangut kingdom. It was during the last of his six attacks on this western region that he perished. Traveling hundreds of miles over grasslands and desert, the expedition team honored the lost Tangut civilization at the hive-like ruins of their royal tombs.

❺ A FINAL DISCOVERY

Alan believes there is no substitute for being there, in person—no matter what the obstacles. On his last day in the field, Alan makes a find: a marker with a message hidden by moss. It's not in any of the books he's read or searchable online. Yet there it was in front of him: one more clue to the last days Genghis Khan. Another step closer to fulfilling his mission.

Warren Caldwell   Hiroshi Hara/A Family Affair Films   Hiroshi Hara/A Family Affair Films

LAND ROVER
ABOVE AND BEYOND

SURE-FOOTED AND TRUSTED

Genghis Khan was a commander of exquisitely skilled horsemen and a shrewd strategist who used every means available in warfare. Crossing the same Ordos Desert terrain, Alan set out to test the rate of travel of the fallen leader's funeral cortege—historically believed to be drawn by horses and camels.

Hiroshi Hara/A Family Affair Films

Mike Pizzio has been a member of the Explorers Club since 2008. He joined Alan's expedition team to run ground operations and experience the thrill of discovery. What he found in Inner Mongolia was not exactly what he expected.

A DETERMINED PATH

WHERE ONE MAN FINDS THE CONFIDENCE TO EXPLORE

What experiences prepared you for this adventure?

I've had an interesting professional life that has exposed me to many potentially dangerous elements: the Mafia, Chinese street gangs, bank robberies, kidnappings, extortions. I've been to Iraq and woken up to mortar attacks, rocket attacks, and small-arms fire. I've been in a variety of military vehicles: Black Hawks, Humvees, Abrams tanks, Stryker Brigade Combat Team vehicles. So, I've traveled under some very extreme conditions.

Through all of this, what has been most important to you?

Integrity. At the end of the day, it's all a person has. I have the experiences, the training, and the knowledge I've gained throughout my life, but all I'm really left with is my integrity. I call it as I see it, and I appreciate other people who act that way.

How did you join Alan's expedition?

Alan needed someone to coordinate set up on the ground and manage the camp sites. The story of Genghis Khan is interesting to me. He had humble beginnings and ended up ruling the largest contiguous empire the world has ever seen. And he didn't have Aristotle as a mentor.

As it turns out, Inner Mongolia is quite a bit different than I expected. It's not as remote and has numerous large road construction

projects. There were places with road conditions that looked difficult. Initially, I would say, "I'm not sure we should go there, guys." But we just raised the car up on its axles, put it in forward, and made it through. I wouldn't have done that with my own SUV.

What driving features are useful in these conditions?

When we were worried about ground clearance, all we had to do was push a button. You could hear the air pumps elevate the vehicle. There was one situation in the Helan Mountains—going through high grass, up over a blind ridge, and down the other side. There's another button for downhill, and that's particularly nice. Generally when you're driving a four-wheel drive downhill you want to maintain a constant speed, with one foot on the brake, one foot on the gas. With that downhill crawl mode*, I didn't have to do much. It took a lot of the guesswork out of it.

Throughout the trip—we covered more than 2,600 miles—I always felt in control. The car's features were well suited to each situation we encountered. And overall it's a very comfortable drive. I own a four-wheel drive and I've driven a lot of four-wheel-drive vehicles: The LR4 is a good combination of a sedan-type vehicle and off-road capability.

What is one of the most memorable experiences of the trip?

When we first arrived at Mountain X, they offered to let us stay in the temple overnight. There we were, inside this temple on a sacred mountain, and bedding down with Buddhas surrounding us. You wake up in the morning and it's a little surreal.

*These systems are not a substitute for driving safely with due care and attention and will not feature under all circumstances, speeds, weather and road conditions, etc. Driver should not assume that these systems will correct errors of judgment in driving. Please consult the owner's manual or your local authorized Land Rover Retailer for more details.

LAND ROVER
ABOVE AND BEYOND

John Rice

"I don't know that we'll find any more or any less than anybody else, but like I always say, you're not going to find anything sitting on a sofa watching TV."
—Mike Pizzio

Warren Caldwell

TO LEARN MORE AND VIEW LAND ROVER VIDEOS, VISIT **youtube.com/landroverusa** TODAY.

Grid Data Results of the Expedition to Ancient Mongolia to Find the Secret Tomb of Chinggis Qa'an

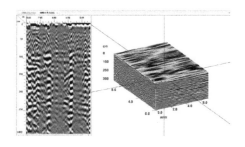

2017 Rev 1

Table of Contents:

- Preamble
    - Background
    - Instruments used make and model, calibration and setup procedures and experience with it, technical associates who accompanied GPR equipment, renting agency contact info. Training courses, companies and instructors we did. Including Geometrics, GSSI, Nico, Scott.
    - Factors known that could influence data such as time constraints, ability to prep survey area, etc.
    - Processes ulitized
- Site patch map by section
- By patch (1-27)
    - Field notes- photo gallery, site geology notes, cultural and community notes such as site frequented by hikers etc., general weather and temperatures daily, ground water
    - Mag 3-D plot
    - GPR 3-D plot
    - Correlation speculation- highlighted anomolies
- Results To date ... Grid Reports Analysis ...
  Highlights ... Grid Summary ...

Preamble: Background...

I believe we have located the secret tomb of CQ on "Mountain X" based on over eight years of research and four expeditions.

CQ died in August of 1227 in the Liu Pan mountains. Our expedition has established the route of Chinggis' funeral cortege to Mountain X (the location is confidential in order to preserve and protect the site for future generations of the public, historians, archeologists and anthropologists.

This report is intended to prove what we already know... without excavation and disturbing the tomb and it's invaluable contents. This grave site is under Mountain X, an important sacred mountain for many many centuries.

The field teams to gather the raw magnetometry and radar data were led by our chief expedition scientists Jerry Griffith (Magnetometry) and Tim Leow (Ground Penetrating Radar). The expedition expresses gratitude to these two leaders and to others participating in the field and as advisors including Stew Lauterbach, Becky Nichols, Chinese experts, Nicholas Tripcevich, Scott Byram, Peter Leach, Dr. Simon Klemperer, Dr. Johan Elverskog and others.

Alan,

Expedition Leader

CONFIDENTIAL. THIS REPORT (Technical Results of the Expedition to Ancient Mongolia to find the secret tomb of Chinggis Qa'an) IS A HIGHLY CONFIDENTIAL DOCUMENT AND DISCLOSURE WITHOUT THE WRITTEN PERMISSION OF THE SACRED MOUNTAIN FOUNDATION WILL SUBJECT THE DISCLOSING PERSON OR ENTITY TO SERIOUS LIABILITY AND COULD RESULT IN IRREMEDIABLE DAMAGE TO THIS IMPORTANT HISTORICAL GRAVESITE.

Technology...GPR/Mag...

We know where CQ is buried...But we have to prove it without digging...yet.

Beside satellite imagery and site inspection, our main tools are GPR (Ground Penetrating Radar) and Mag (Magnetometry), both ideal archeologial tools to confirm the underground burial site. Together, they combine their advantages, reduce their limitations, and minimize their separate disadvantages.

Magnetometry

The Grad601 is a high-resolution fluxgate gradiometer, used for measuring minute variations in the magnetic field that are caused by hidden anomalies in the ground, such as archaeological features, pipes, cables or unexploded ordnance (UXO).The full system includes a data logger, a battery cassette, and either one or two Grad-01-1000L sensors mounted on a rigid carrying bar. Prominently used in archeological projects to delineate large and prominent earthworks but not useable to locate human remains. Soil conditions are important. Also magnetometry is good to locate small objects since readings same effect as large objects particularly when sensors operated close to ground. Detectable anomalies that can and have been found underground at other sites include knives, barrels, belt buckles, large numbers of bodies (anaerobic situations), tunnels, and caves.

Notes: "Noise" to be avoided include buildings, bridges, geologic features, rocks, metal structures , high levels of magnetic energy, operator accessories like cell phones, buckles, keys...Best to test general soil conditions in area for comparison.

Ground Penetrating Radar

The SIR® 4000 is GSSI's first high-performance GPR data acquisition system designed to operate with analog and digital antennas. This evolutionary step allows true versatility and flexibility by supporting a wide range of users, beginner to advanced, in numerous applications. The SIR 4000 incorporates advanced display modes and filtering capabilities for 'in-the-field' processing and imaging. Fully integrated, the system provides a simple user interface, plug-and-play GPS integration, and convenient data transfer options. GPR provides the only true "wave" method and different from all other underground testing methods. Dialectic conduction varies with different materials involved.
The higher frequency (we used 400 MGHZ, the smaller the wave length, the better to "see" smaller items underground. CQ's tomb may include many small items—artifacts, horse accessories, tools, weapons, etc. While 50 meter penetration possible, most of our GPR depth up to about 20 meters. Our vendor and Forensic Geophysics investigates clandestine graves in many contexts...and are useful for our CQ tomb analysis. Possible analysis techniques include horizontal scale and distance based, editing data files including channel blending, making weaker targets brighter with color changes, range gain, and relativity, depth analysis with time zero and migration techniques, and noise reduction including background removal, stacking, frequency filtering, and deconvolution

Notes: GPR equipment works best with low surface conductivity as in ice, snow, dry sandy soil, dry concrete but not in salt water, clay, and construction debris. Best GPR requires good ground coupling —flat, paved surfaces without grasses. plants, debris, rocks, etc. Electronic radio interference and cell phones reduce effectiveness.

Raw data processing:

GPR

1. Time zero
2. Background removal
3. Range gain (auto 10 pts)
4. IIR Filter (550/300 4pole)
5. Range gain (Exponential-curve)

Mag

1. Clip to +_100

Site Grid Map

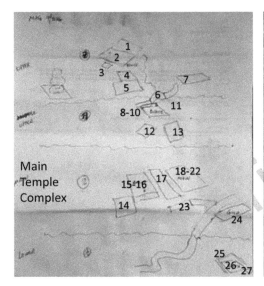

1 Tent city Upper
2 Tent city Lower
3 Tent city pit
4 Tent city ruins
5 Tent city grass patch
6 Tibet temple road above
7 Tibet temple brick flat
8 Tibet temple north wall outside
9 Tibet temple inside Center
10 Tibet temple inside right
11 Tibet temple surround
12 Tibet temple lower front west
13 Tibet temple lower front east
14 West temple patio
15 West temple east
16 West temple west
17 Road between west
18 Main middle west
19 Main middle middle
20 Main middle lower
22 Main lower east
23 Main road in front
24 Gold building
25 South temple surround
26 South temple inside
27 South temple outside

The 27 grids from the expedition's radar and magnetometry data constitute 2% of the entire potential gravesite of Mountain X.

1 Tent city Upper

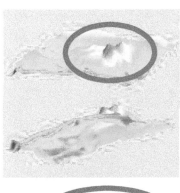

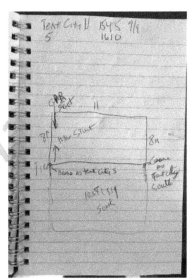

Filename: tent city repeat north.xcp
Direction of 1st Traverse: 0 deg
Collection Method: ZigZag
Sensors: 2 @ 1.00 m spacing.
Grid Size: 8 m x 11 m
X Interval: 0.125 m
Y Interval: 0.5 m

Clipped +_100 nT

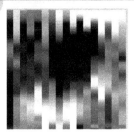

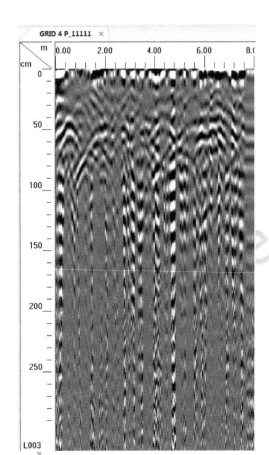

GRID 4 P_11111

L003

Profile 3 of 12

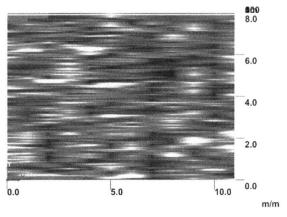

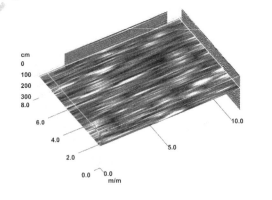

2 Tent city Lower

Filename: tent city south repeat.xcp
Direction of 1st Traverse: 0 deg
Collection Method: ZigZag
Sensors: 2 @ 1.00 m spacing.
Grid Size: 11 m x 10 m
X Interval: 0.125 m
Y Interval: 0.5 m

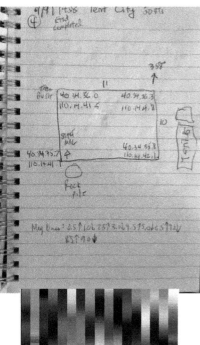

Clipped +_100 nT

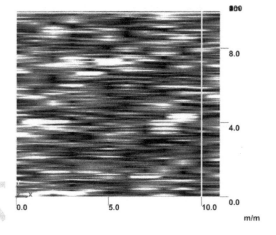

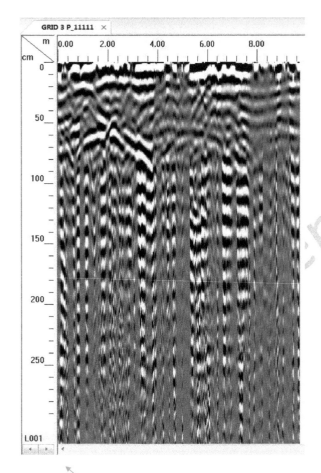

Profile 1 of 12

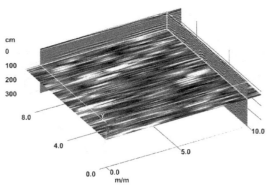

3 Tent city pit-GPR NA

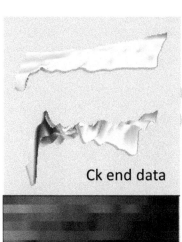

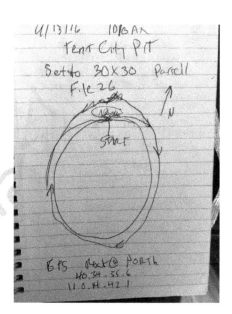

Clipped +_100 nT

4 Tent City ruins-GPR NA

Filename: tents ruins below.xcp
Direction of 1st Traverse: 270 deg
Collection Method: Parallel
Sensors: 2 @ 1.00 m spacing
Grid Size: 6 m x 10 m
X Interval: 0.125 m
Y Interval: 0.5 m

Ck end data

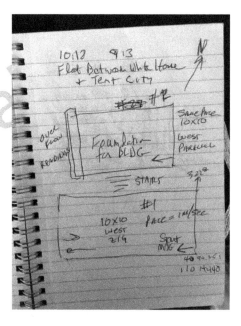

Clipped +_100 nT

5 Tent City grass patch

Filename: tents below flat.xcp
Direction of 1st Traverse: 270 deg
Collection Method: ZigZag
Sensors: 2 @ 1.00 m spacing.
Grid Size: 10 m x 10 m
X Interval: 0.125 m
Y Interval: 0.5 m

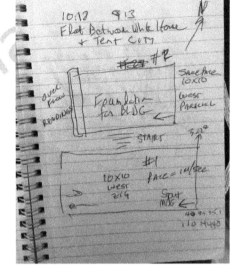

Clipped +_100 nT

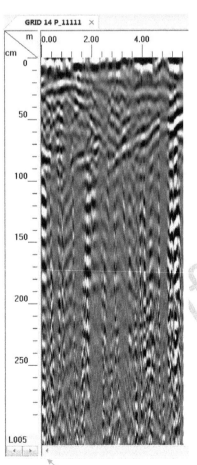

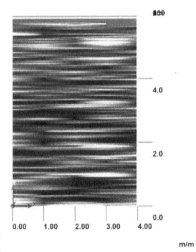

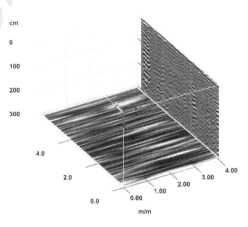

Profile 5 of 5

108

6 Tibet temple road above

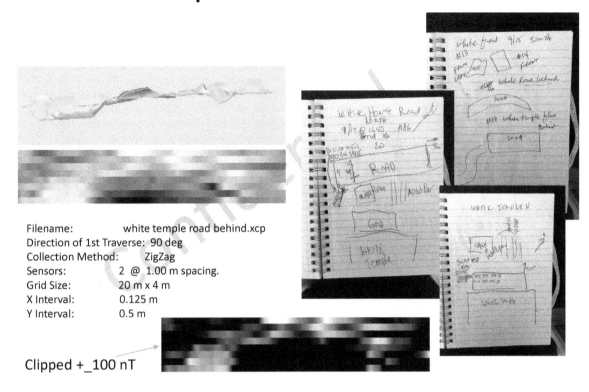

Filename: white temple road behind.xcp
Direction of 1st Traverse: 90 deg
Collection Method: ZigZag
Sensors: 2 @ 1.00 m spacing.
Grid Size: 20 m x 4 m
X Interval: 0.125 m
Y Interval: 0.5 m

Clipped +_100 nT

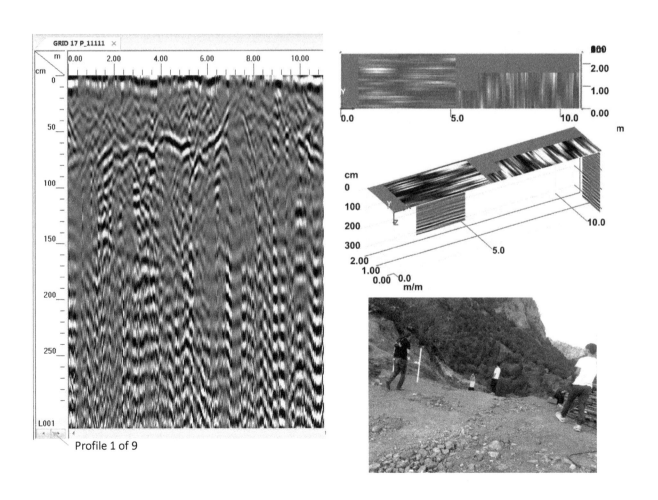

GRID 17 P_11111

Profile 1 of 9

7 Tibet temple brick flat

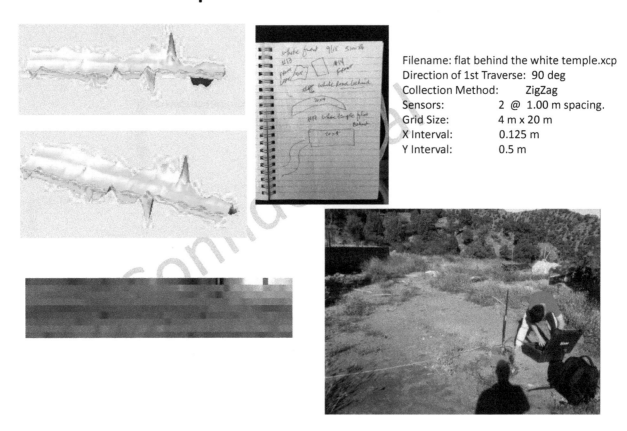

Filename: flat behind the white temple.xcp
Direction of 1st Traverse: 90 deg
Collection Method: ZigZag
Sensors: 2 @ 1.00 m spacing.
Grid Size: 4 m x 20 m
X Interval: 0.125 m
Y Interval: 0.5 m

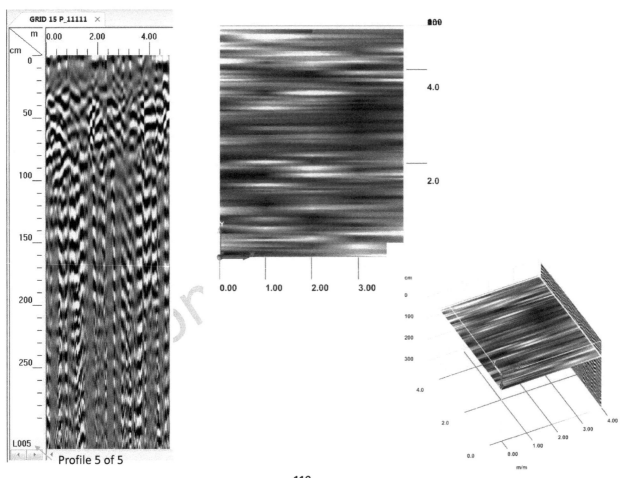

GRID 15 P_11111

Profile 5 of 5

8 Tibet temple north wall outside

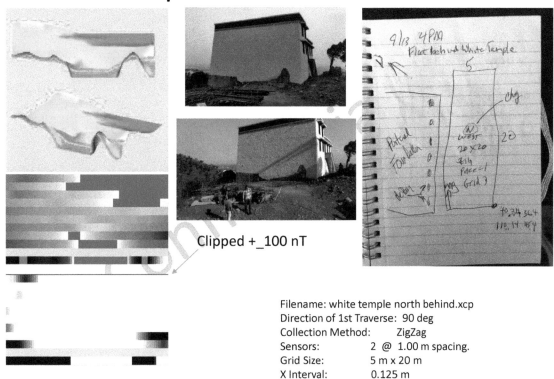

Clipped +_100 nT

Filename: white temple north behind.xcp
Direction of 1st Traverse: 90 deg
Collection Method: ZigZag
Sensors: 2 @ 1.00 m spacing.
Grid Size: 5 m x 20 m
X Interval: 0.125 m
Y Interval: 0.5 m

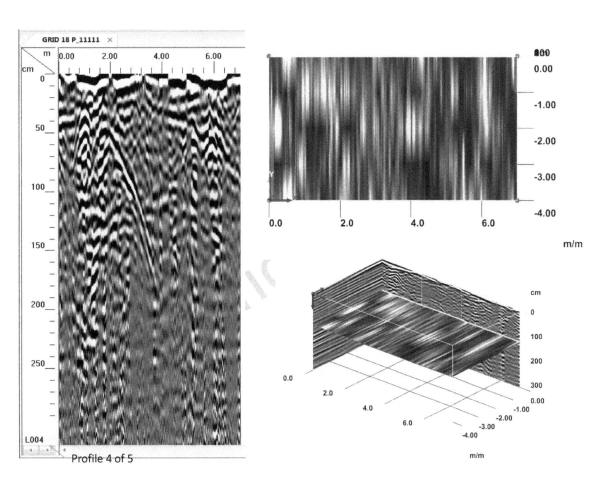

Profile 4 of 5

9 Tibet temple Inside Center

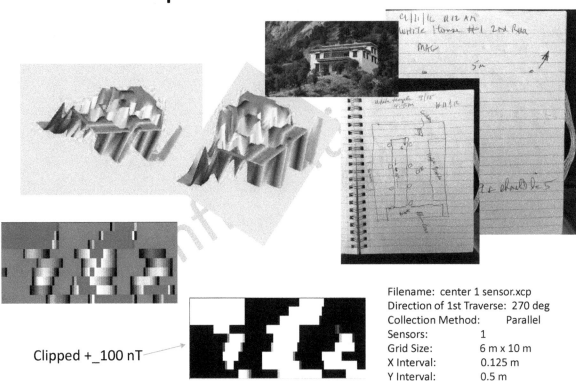

Clipped +_100 nT

Filename: center 1 sensor.xcp
Direction of 1st Traverse: 270 deg
Collection Method: Parallel
Sensors: 1
Grid Size: 6 m x 10 m
X Interval: 0.125 m
Y Interval: 0.5 m

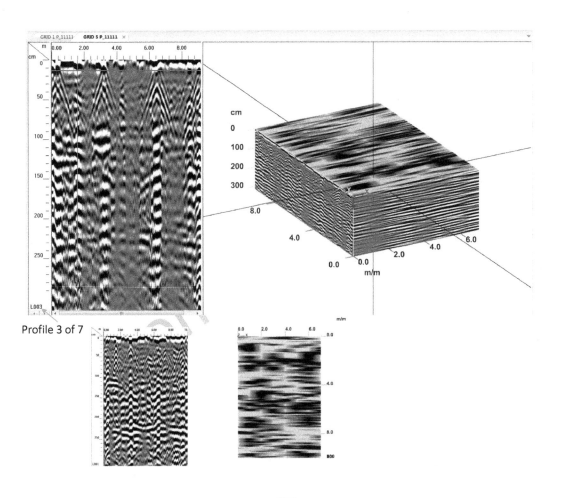

Profile 3 of 7

10 Tibet temple inside right

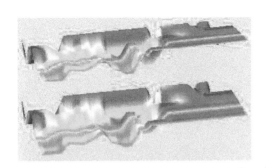

right 1 sensor.xcp
Direction of 1st Traverse: 0 deg
Collection Method: Parallel
Sensors: 1
Grid Size: 3 m x 10 m
X Interval: 0.125 m
Y Interval: 0.5 m

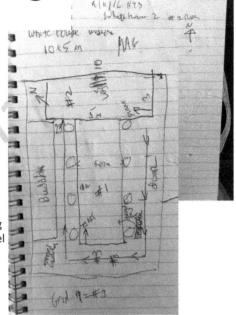

Clipped +_100 nT

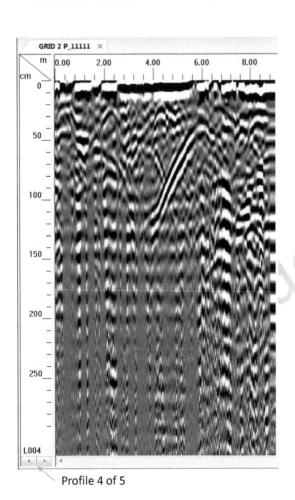

Profile 4 of 5

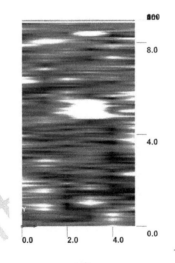

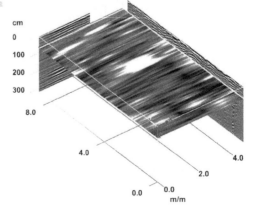

11 Tibet temple surround- GPR NA

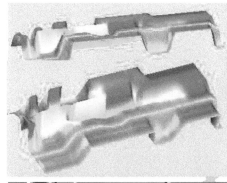

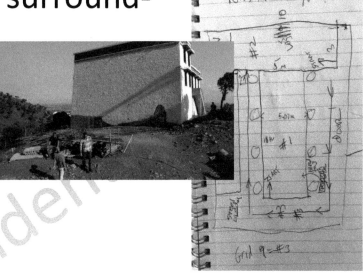

Clipped +_100 nT

Filename: surround inside white temple.xcp
Direction of 1st Traverse: 0 deg
Collection Method: ZigZag
Sensors: 2 @ 1.00 m spacing.
Grid Size: 2 m x 30 m but not concatenated
X Interval: 0.125 m
Y Interval: 0.5 m

12 Tibet temple lower front west

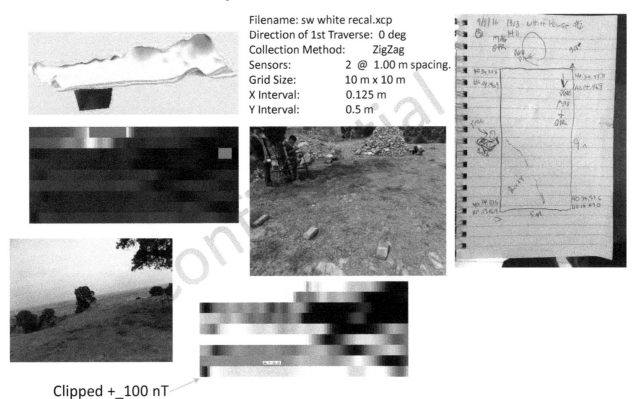

Filename: sw white recal.xcp
Direction of 1st Traverse: 0 deg
Collection Method: ZigZag
Sensors: 2 @ 1.00 m spacing.
Grid Size: 10 m x 10 m
X Interval: 0.125 m
Y Interval: 0.5 m

Clipped +_100 nT

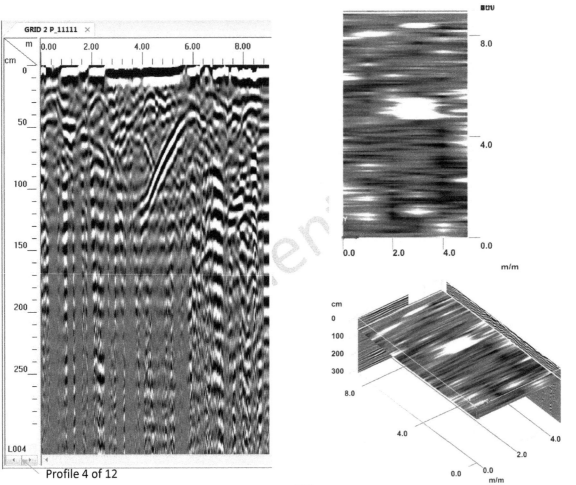

GRID 2 P_11111

Profile 4 of 12

13 Tibet temple lower front east

Filename: se white recal.xcp
Direction of 1st Traverse: 0 deg
Collection Method: ZigZag
Sensors: 2 @ 1.00 m
spacing.
Grid Size: 10 m x 10 m
X Interval: 0.125 m
Y Interval: 0.5 m

Clipped +_100 nT

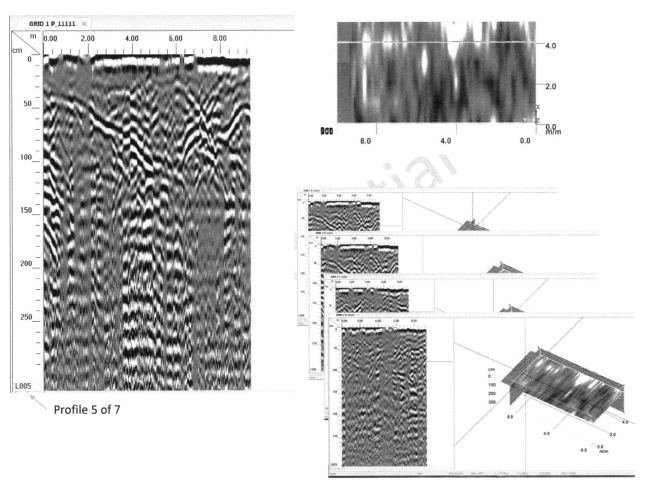

Profile 5 of 7

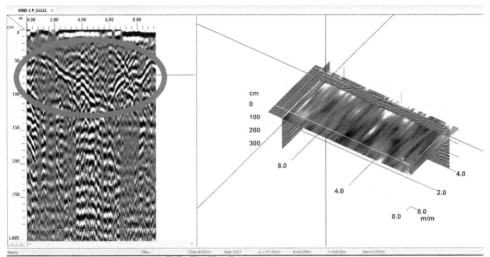

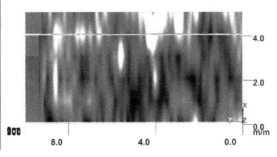

14 West temple patio

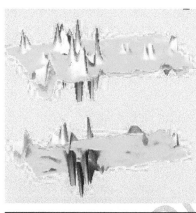

Filename: west temple patio.xcp
Direction of 1st Traverse: 0 deg
Collection Method: ZigZag
Sensors: 2 @ 1.00 m spacing.
Grid Size: 20 m x 20 m
X Interval: 0.125 m
Y Interval: 0.5 m

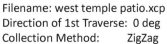

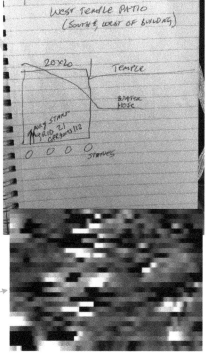

Clipped +_100 nT

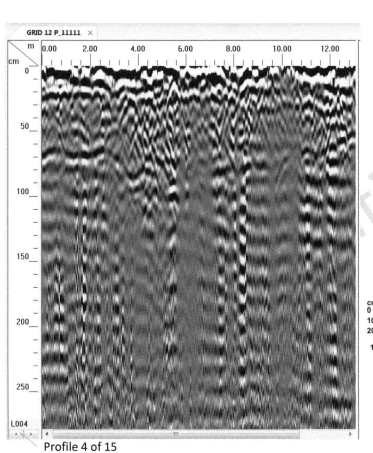

Profile 4 of 15

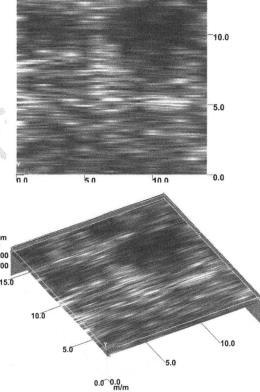

15 West temple east

Clipped +_100 nT

Filename: west temple first half.xcp
Direction of 1st Traverse: 0 deg
Collection Method: ZigZag
Sensors: 2 @ 1.00 m spacing.
Grid Size: 10 m x 20 m
X Interval: 0.125 m
Y Interval: 0.5 m

16 West temple west

west temple 2nd half redo.xcp
Direction of 1st Traverse: 0 deg
Collection Method: ZigZag
Sensors: 2 @ 1.00 m spacing.
Grid Size: 10 m x 20 m
X Interval: 0.125 m
Y Interval: 0.5 m

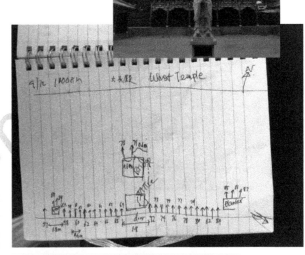

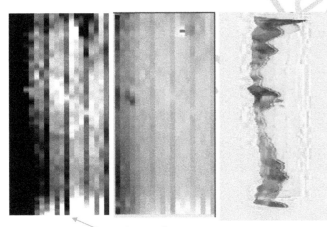

Clipped +_100 nT

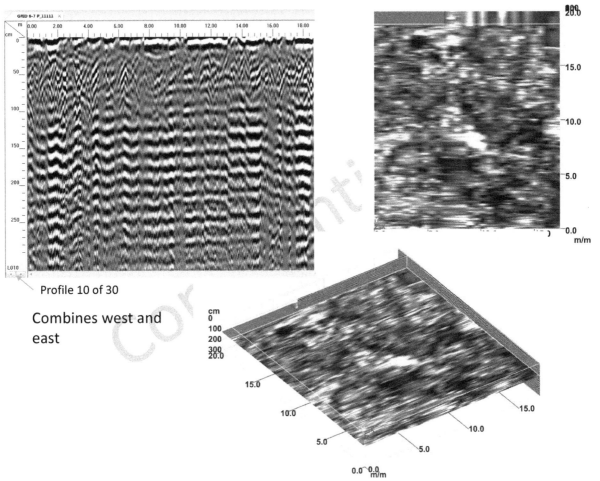

Profile 10 of 30

Combines west and east

17 Road between west & main temple

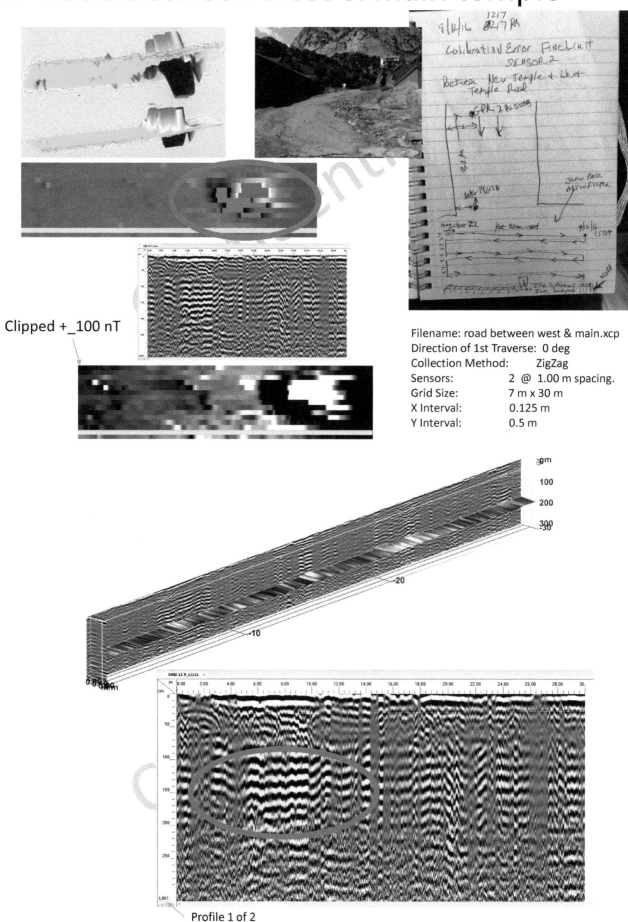

Clipped +_100 nT

Filename: road between west & main.xcp
Direction of 1st Traverse: 0 deg
Collection Method: ZigZag
Sensors: 2 @ 1.00 m spacing.
Grid Size: 7 m x 30 m
X Interval: 0.125 m
Y Interval: 0.5 m

Profile 1 of 2

18 Main middle west

Clipped +_100 nT

Filename: main west middle.xcp
Direction of 1st Traverse: ? deg
Collection Method: Parallel
Sensors: 1
Grid Size: 10 m x 10 m
X Interval: 0.125 m
Y Interval: 0.5 m

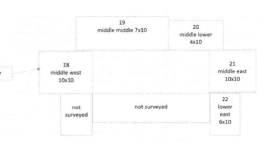

Confidential

19 Main middle middle

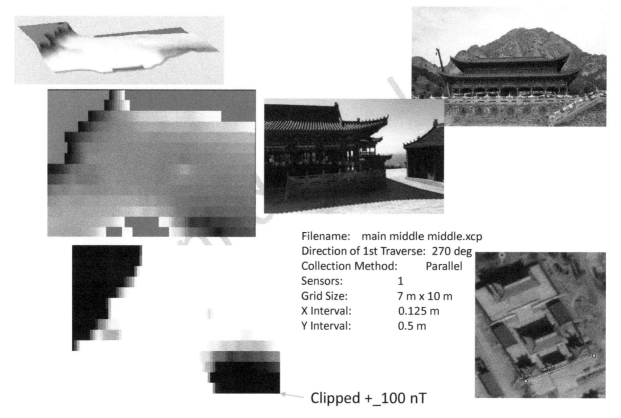

Filename: main middle middle.xcp
Direction of 1st Traverse: 270 deg
Collection Method: Parallel
Sensors: 1
Grid Size: 7 m x 10 m
X Interval: 0.125 m
Y Interval: 0.5 m

Clipped +_100 nT

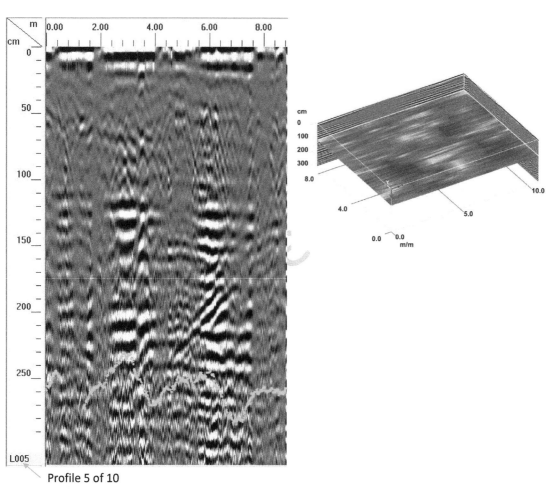

Profile 5 of 10

20 Main middle lower

Filename: main middle lower.xcp
Direction of 1st Traverse: 270 deg
Collection Method: Parallel
Sensors: 1
Grid Size: 4 m x 10 m
X Interval: 0.125 m
Y Interval: 0.5 m

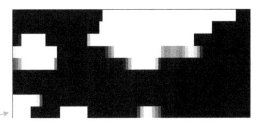

Clipped +_100 nT

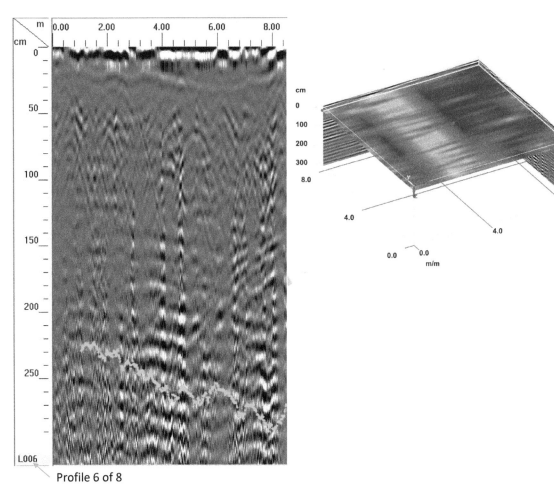

Profile 6 of 8

21 Main middle east

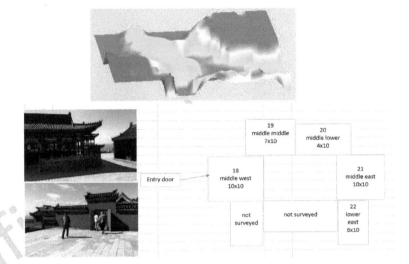

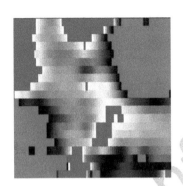

Filename: main east middle.xcp
Direction of 1st Traverse: 270 deg
Collection Method: Parallel
Sensors: 1
Grid Size: 10 m x 10 m
X Interval: 0.125 m
Y Interval: 0.5 m

Clipped +_100 nT

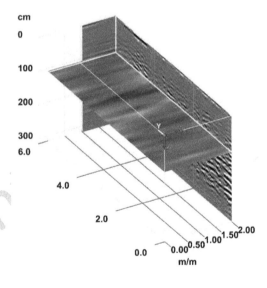

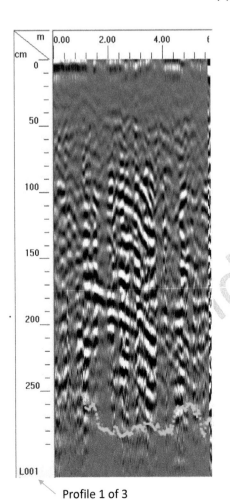

Profile 1 of 3

22 Main temple lower east

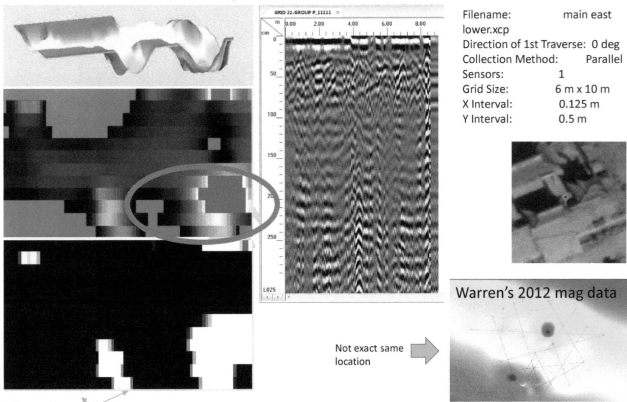

Filename: main east lower.xcp
Direction of 1st Traverse: 0 deg
Collection Method: Parallel
Sensors: 1
Grid Size: 6 m x 10 m
X Interval: 0.125 m
Y Interval: 0.5 m

Warren's 2012 mag data

Not exact same location

Clipped +_100 nT Profile 3 of 12

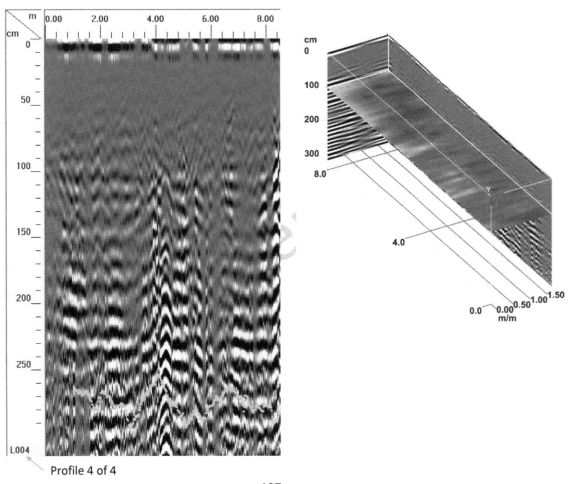

Profile 4 of 4

23 Main temple road in front

Filename: main road in front x5.xcp
Direction of 1st Traverse: 90 deg
Collection Method: Parallel
Sensors: 1
Grid Size: 20 (3) m x 20 m
X Interval: 0.125 m
Y Interval: 0.5 m

Clipped +_100 nT

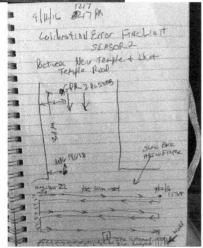

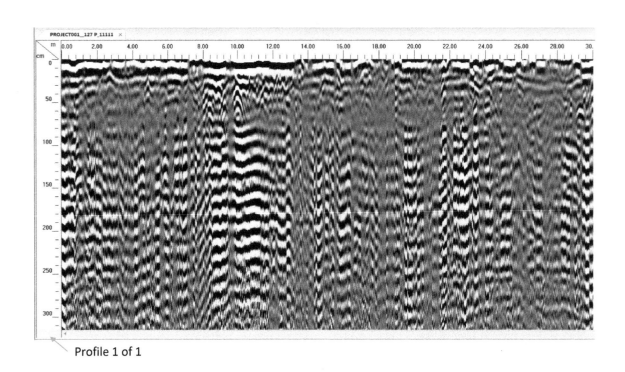

Profile 1 of 1

24 Gold building

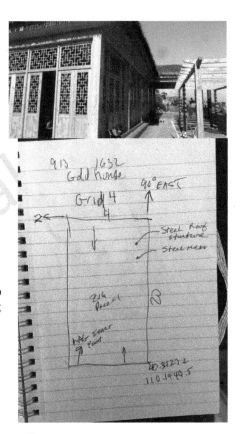

Filename: gold building 0913.xcp
Direction of 1st Traverse: 90 deg
Collection Method: ZigZag
Sensors: 2 @ 1.00 m spacing.
Grid Size: 6 m x 20 m
X Interval: 0.125 m
Y Interval: 0.5 m

Clipped +_100 nT

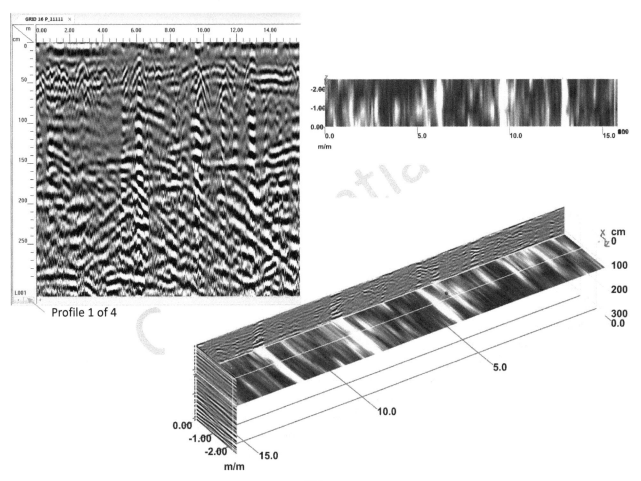

Profile 1 of 4

25 South temple surround –GPR NA

Filename: south temple surround.xcp
Direction of 1st Traverse: 270 deg
Collection Method: Parallel
Sensors: 2 @ 1.00 m spacing.
Grid Size: 10 m x 10 m
X Interval: 0.125 m
Y Interval: 0.5 m

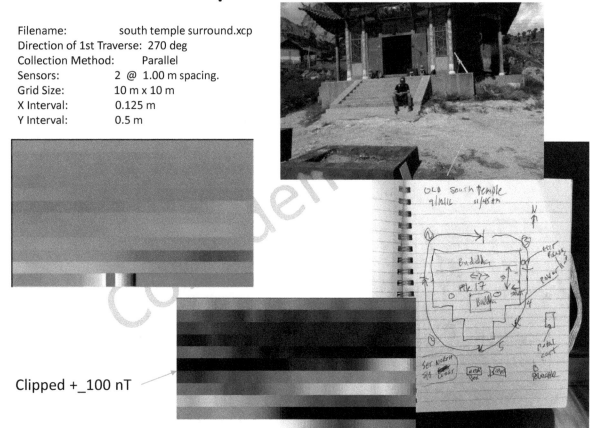

Clipped +_100 nT

26 South temple inside

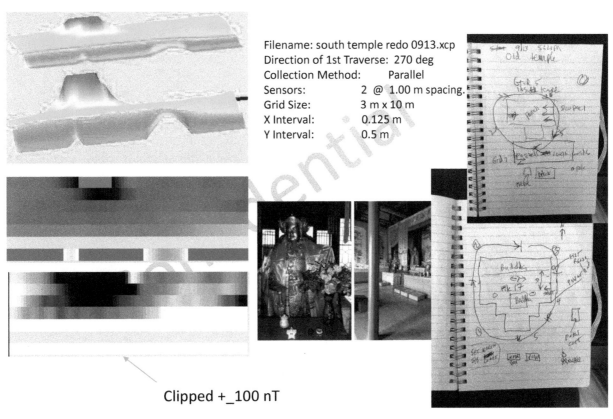

Filename: south temple redo 0913.xcp
Direction of 1st Traverse: 270 deg
Collection Method: Parallel
Sensors: 2 @ 1.00 m spacing.
Grid Size: 3 m x 10 m
X Interval: 0.125 m
Y Interval: 0.5 m

Clipped +_100 nT

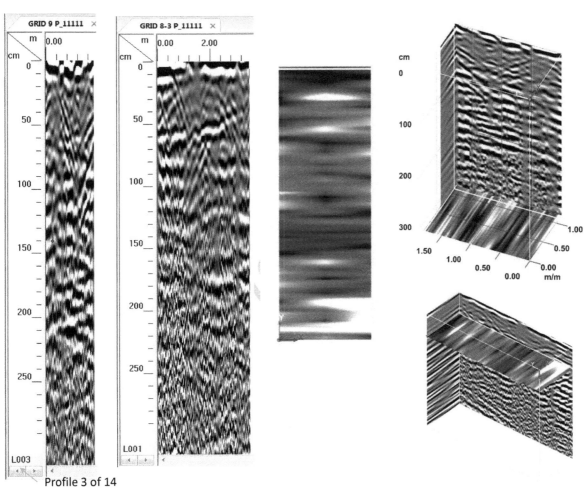

Profile 3 of 14

27 South temple outside

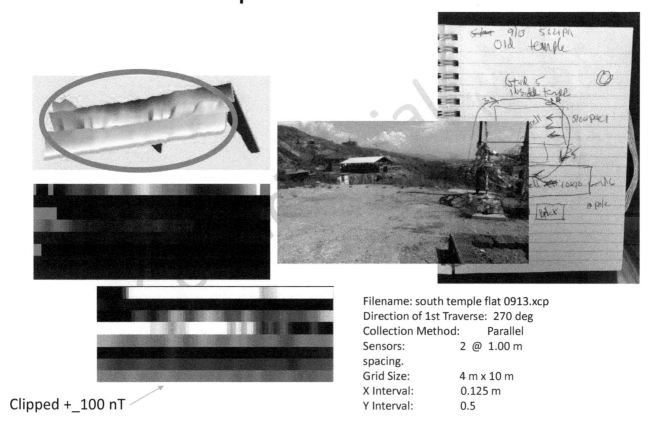

Filename: south temple flat 0913.xcp
Direction of 1st Traverse: 270 deg
Collection Method: Parallel
Sensors: 2 @ 1.00 m spacing.
Grid Size: 4 m x 10 m
X Interval: 0.125 m
Y Interval: 0.5

Clipped +_100 nT

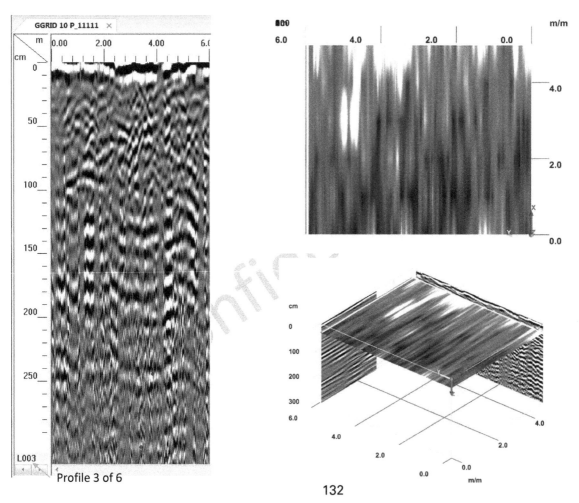

Profile 3 of 6

Highlights:

1. Adequate Data gathering operations are of course of primary importance but the most difficult step is analysis of the data for which special knowledge, experience and practice are critical.
2. Environmental considerations and ground materials key to successful testing and should be analyzed for comparison with target items and materials
3. Actual ground-truthing tests may well be required.
4. Anomalies were discovered that could be the contents of the tomb of CQ.
5. We attempted to collect data in the same area where previous data showed existing anomalies.
6. We avoided grids with obvious anomalies from new construction and current site development.
7. Our test equipment (fluxgate gradiometer of magnetometry and SIR 4000 for GPR) were ideal, especially since customs and import requirements were avoided by acquisitions in China.
8. Review by highly qualified archeologist experienced with the use of magnetometry and radar is recommended.
9. Our process was to first analyze the GPR data and then confirm "hotspots" with Mag data. The analysis for GPR and Mag data are completely different and Mag is useful to discover underground ferrous artifacts. Our team performed a major task in organizing and comparing the processed Mag and GPR data... As illustrated in this report "Technical Results of the Expedition to Ancient Mongolia to Find the Secret Tomb of Chinggis Qa'an". An experienced, knowledgeableexpert is vital to make our final conclusions.
10. Our science expedition team recommends special expert review of data and processing (both 2D and 3D) of all grids.
11. The proposed "pseudo" gravity and edge detection techniques suggested by Stanford University should be pursued.

Grid Reports:

1. Grids 1 and 2 Tent City Upper and Lower. Subsurface anomalies collocated GPR and Mag.
2. Grids 1, 2, 13, 17, 22 & 27 are all higher potential tomb-sites and should be re-reviewed carefully to determine more clearly the exact nature of the anomalies.
3. Grids 1 & 13 anomalies may be a large bolder or granite floor.
4. Grid 17 mag has no explanation for this except a possible grave.
5. Grid 5 Tent City Grass Patch contains subsurface anomalies, both reflective and ferrous, and are in the same place for both GPR and Mag results.
6. Grid 6 Temple Road Above (GPR Profile 11 anomaly and Mag Black Box in 3 places);
7. Grid 7 Tibet Temple (GPR difficult—too much grass and debris but white streaks showing high reflection...Mag shows possible trench and red anomaly),
8. Grid 8 Tibet Temple north wall outside. GPR 2 meter long image; Mag blips probably are scaffolding and "metal" in wall.
9. Grid 10 Temple Inside Right. Mag- no results; GPR- possible artifacts.
10. Grid 12 Tibet Temple Lower West. GPR stingers profile 3 an 4. Mag readings are possible rock pile and bench.
11. Grid 13 Tibet Temple Lower Front East. GSSI advisor picks selects grid 13 as gris with the most possibilities. GPR 5 profiles could possible be 15 foot grave cavity. Mag shows collocated anomaly.
12. Grid 14 West Temple Patio GPR and Mag anomalies that may be construction elements since 15 foot construction material or space underneath floor.
13. Grids 15, 16 West Temple east and west inside. GPR Profile 10, 12. Mag shows unexplained anomaly.
14. Grid 17 Road Between West and Main Temple. Mag's large anomaly correlates with GPR Profile. Mag anomaly approximately 12 feet by 12 feet per magnetometry.
15. Grids 18, 19, 20, 21 difficult to co-relate magnetometry and GPR but magnetometry shows large anomaly possibly from wall or foundation adjoining GRID.
16. Grid 22 mag data may correlate to Warren's 2012 data... Main Temple Inside Lower East. GPR profiles 23, 24, 25. Mag high readings probably metal. Area tested is co-related to Caldwell Magnetometry "hotspot".
17. Grid 23...GPR image had significant face changes at the top. Additional processing needed.
18. Grid 24..."Gold" colored building could be interference with metal roof and overhang affecting both mag and GPR results.
19. Grid 25...12 foot long man-made anomaly red stripe. Likely to be from surround data gathering and adjoining wall. Artifacts unlikely.
20. Grid 26...Anomalies shown probably from linear interference from Buddha and warrior statue and alter but not building posts.
21. Grid 27 should be subjected to further analysis by expert in spite of metal structure. Grid 27 has similar imagery to Grid 13 but could be alluvial fan or man made underground structure. Grid 27 first useable plateau for burial of artifacts on SE Mountain X.

Grid Report Summary:

- Underground anomalies exist in all 27 grids tested on site with Magnetometry and Ground Penetrating Radar.

- The anomalies include a typical GPR radar image of a grave and innumerable examples of artifacts that could be items known to be a part of a CQ gravesite.

- The most prominent anomalies are in Grids 1, 2, 13, 17 , 22, 27.

Jerry, magnetometer, site buildings and Mountain X.

THE HUNTER AND THE HUNTED

*THE SEARCH FOR THE SECRET BURIAL OF CHINGGIS QA'AN**

The 2016 Mountain X
Expedition.

"A *true* Story"

*A.K.A. Erroneously Genghis Khan.

THE MYSTERY

Genghis Khan is a collosus of history and revolutionary warrior who conquered extraordinary swaths of land from his native Mongolia, nearly taking over Asia and Europe by horseback.

After his death in 1227, Khan (more accurately pronounced Chinggis Qa'an) was secretly buried by his elite band of troops. But the location of Qa'an's grave is one of the great mysteries of our time, and bands of treasure hunters and many others including Marco Polo have been hunting for the missing tomb for centuries, and discovering its location would be considered one of the most significant archaelogical findings in history.

Armed with next generation underground testing equipment and a new team of explorers, our expedition to find Chinngis Qa'an's tomb will lead to the preservation of history's most famous undiscoverd vault, yielding the legednary conquerors silver casket, weapons, horse guards, servants , vital DNA and the corpse of Qa'an himself.

Along with scientific research, we've joined forces with True.Ink, the revial of an iconic adventure magazine, whose editors will document our search for Chinggis Qa'an's remains, and bring to life the final days of the legendary warrior through an innovative, educational, multimedia microsite and platform.

MOUNTAIN X

After research conducted over nearly a decade, we believe we have isolated a new location for Chinggis Qa'an's final resting place. The location is based not only on physical evidence—specifically, anomalies isolated under the gravestie we call Mountain X, including at least three principles.

1. Chinggis Qa'an and his family along with their Shaman advisors were determined to keep his burial place secret, and the location of the tomb must reflect that effort.

2. Chinggis Qa'an was a follower of Mongolian Shamanism and was governed by their advice and support; therefore, his burial place must conform to the following Mongolian Shaman requirements: (a)He must be buried in a place consistent with shamanistic funeral practices; (b) He must be buried promptly (some claim within fourteen days of death) to deter evil forces from invading the corpse; and (c) He must be buried strategically to carry out his afterlife mission—namely, protecting the Mongolian people and to "bring the whole world under his sword," particularly Southern China.

3. Chinggis Qa'an and his successors were masters of deception in military tactics. The actual tomb location was hidden. Anyone looking for the grave has been intentionally deceived as to the location. The location therefore must reflect significant deceptions.

This fall, equipped with advanced magnotometers and new underground testing equipment, we will return to Mountain X to achieve at least the following six objectives:

1.) To confirm the location of the tomb.
2.) To obtain insight information and testing for site excavation application.
3.) To use higher resolution magnetometry equipment and other testing equipment including underground penetrating x-ray, electrical impulses, and special satellite imagery.
4.) To complete intensive interviews with local residents and review records with local archivists
5.) To physically map alternative burial sites on the mountain.
6.) To protect and conserve the site.

We believe our expedition will result in not only the discovery of Chinggis Qa'an's tomb, but lead to a greater historical and cultural understanding of the controversial conqueror and his empire. Here's why:

1.) It would be inappropriate and illegal to excavate on Mountain X. Therefore, we need to use higher resolution magnotemeters to expand on previous anomalies to create a more compelling case before Chinese, University, and UN heritage archaeologists who could excavate.

2.) The tomb itself is a historical treasure trove. Historians believe it includes the silver casket, weapons, gold and silver objects, horse guards and servants, personal possessions, and innumerable other artifacts related to Chinggis Qa'an. Since the Tomb has never been exploited by anyone, it would be an invaluable pristine resource for basic research for Scientists, especially archeologists, historians, and treasure conservationists.

3.) The Project envisions a major museum facility for the general public to celebrate the history of Chinggis Qa'an (comparable or even in cooperation with the existing Mausoleum in Inner Mongolia) and a research facility for visiting and residing scholars. The facility would also prepare traveling exhibits for use at other museums throughout the world, and be a model of protection, conservation, and appropriate access and appreciation.

Alan Nichols is a distinguished explorer, attorney, expert on sacred mountains and burial sites, and has spent many years researching the life of Qa'an and searching for his tomb. He has trekked to the location three times, and established a network of supporters, scientists, and allies in the States, China, and the geophysics and other departments at Stanford University. Dr. Nichols, a published author and leader of 9 Explorers Club flag expeditions, also served as the 42nd president of the Explorer's Club, and has earned many awards and distinctions, among them a first: bicycling the entire Silk Web (Silk Road) from Istanbul, Turkey to Xian, China.

Established nearly a decade ago, the Mamont Foundation has been supporting a number of high-profile programs to promote the advancement of scientific research around the planet and the development of a sustainable society.

Founded by philanthropist Frederik Paulsen, an honorary director of the Explorer's Club and chairman of the board at Ferring Pharmaceuticals, the Mamont Foundation is a partner in Mountain X, and will assist in the scientific pursuit of identifying the missing tomb. Along with promoting research into the Polar Arctic, Paulsen has been an intrepid explorer, soaring through the skies from Alaska to Russia in an Ultralight plane, and venturing 14,000 feet underwater to the seabed at the Northpole.

Damien Leloup
Director of Paleontology Institute, Northern China, TEC Fellow.

Warren Caldwell
Geophysics Doctorate, Underground testing expert, Stanford University.

Johan Elverskog
Professor of Mongolian history, originator of exploration approach.

Yang Fan
China liaison, translator, transportation, TEC Member.

Tom Cromwell
Medical Consultant, TEC Member.

Frederik Paulsen
Sponsor, Polar explorer, 1st to the 8 poles, TEC Fellow

Steven Schwankert
TEC Member and China Chapter Chair

Becky Nichols
Logistics, TEC Member.

Alan Nichols, Leader
TEC Fellow, TEC 42 President.

This includes only those traveling with the expedition but not the critically important Core Team Members and Advisory Team Members.

No expedition is true exploration unless it's shared with the public and anyone interested. True Magazine has taken on this vital role.

In the 1930's and 40's, True Magazine was the leading adventure periodical in the nation, where writers like Ernest Hemingway and Explorer's Club members Roy Chapman Andrews and Peter Freuchen were constant contributors. Last year, True was revived by New York Times bestselling author and award-winning documentary producer Geoffrey Gray , and now powerd by a team of multimedia storytellers.

Along with documenting the expedition, True will take on the logistical planning, create a digital life for the project, plan events to help promote the expedition. True will also accompany the research team to create and publish a multimedia narrative about the last days of Chinggis Qa'an, parsing fact from fiction and tracing the last steps of the historic conqueror. Already, True has devoted resources towards the expedition, catologuing materials, assembling the team and preparing for on the gorund efforts when the expedition lands in China this fall.

THE HUNTER & HUNTED

Summoning The Spirit of Adventure

1. WHAT WE ACHIEVED

After months of planning, the Sacred Mountain Foundation and journalism team of *True.Ink* were able to capture close to 80 hours of remarkable, documentary-style footage at the highest level.

With a barebones crew, we isolated key characters, documented dramatic moments, and published previews in major outlets like The Huffington Post. We achieved our mission of getting the raw footage needed to shape Sacred Mountain Foundation's quest to not only uncover the location of Chinggis Qa'an's tomb, and now we have the chance to use the story as a pilot for a video series that can inspire young explorers.

2. WHERE WE ARE

Despite a treasure trove of footage, until the technical data is analyzed and reconfirmed by internationally recognized experts, it's unlikely national networks will invest heavily in a specialized series. We have enough material to start editing a limited digital series, showcasing the spirit of adventure in partnership with Mamont Foundation and promote other explorers.

3. OUR OPENING

While television once carried the most impact, our media world is changing rapidly. Most pertinent to the CQ project is the rise of short form, serialized video projects and podcasts.

The benefit of short form video is the programs are designed to be watched on mobile devices. They are far cheaper to produce, quicker to make and ideal for sharing on social media.

Moreover, everyone from traditional outlets like Smithsonian, to upstarts with large digital audiences like Vox are always amenable to sharing this kind of video content and promote Mamont and the spirit of adventure.

4. OUR ADVANTAGES

The material and tale are natural for short form serialization, to be produced in concert with a major digital outlet hungry for video content.

Moreover, we have an additional benefit of the growth of *True.Ink*. Over the past year, True has grown its audience to over 100k e-mail subscribers, and stands to crack the 200k subscriber mark by the end of next year.

As our audience grows larger, we have the ability to attract an advertiser willing to finance the cost of editing, marketing and release.

5. OUR OPTIONS

Irrespective of expert findings, we can now edit, produce and distribute a short, social media friendly video series – perhaps twelve episodes - at three minutes each-in concert with a lead sponsor and media partner.

Pros:
We could plan a release for the fall of next year, have full control of video content, and use an integrated micro-sites within True to inspire a younger generation of explorers.

Cons:
Our distribution will be more targeted yet perhaps not as big. We'd need to find a brand sponsor to underwrite the cost of editing and marketing.

6. OUR RECOMMENDATION

Depending on the findings, we believe the tale, footage and material is too strong not to pursue a short video series.

We also believe the video content could live on a more developed micro-site that fosters discussion on CQ and also celebrates the work or ongoing expeditions of explorers around the world.

Unlike the footage we performed in the field, thanks to our sponsors and donated services from friends, we'd need a budget to properly execute the editing, sound, distribution, marketing, sales, syndication and release of this special project.

Knitted together, we believe CQ could also be a contender for festival release.

POSTSCRIPT X
AUTHOR PUBLICATIONS AND EXPLORATIONS
BIOGRAPHY OF HUNTER

PERSONAL EDUCATION

B.A., L.L.B., and J.D., Stanford University, Graduated Magna Cum Laude; Phi Beta Kappa; Stanford Law Review, Board of Editors; Doctor of Science (D.S.), California College of Podiatric Medicine (Honorary)

Attended schools in Seattle, Washington; Redwood City, California; Pocatello, Idaho; New York City, New York; Falls Church, Virginia; Princeton, New Jersey; Idaho State University.

SACRED MOUNTAINS, CYCLING THE SILK WEB, AND EXPLORATION

Appointed as goodwill Ambassador to several countries in connection with a round-the-world sacred mountain journey by the Board of Supervisors of the City and County of San Francisco and the Board of Directors of the San Francisco Council of Churches

First westerner to circumambulate Mt. Kailas in Southwestern Tibet (after Chinese occupation)

First person (with Keith Brown) to bicycle 3300 miles through Central Asia (from Urumchi, Xinjiang to Lhassa, Tibet) in the Pamir, Kunlun, Korakorum, Trans-Himalayan and Himalayan Mountains and across Tibet

First person (with Shan Nichols) to bicycle 2300 miles on the Silk Road from Ashkabad, Turkmenistan by way of Bohhara, Khiva, Samarkand, Tashikent, Bishtek, and Torugunt Pass in Uzbekistan, Tajikistan, Kyrgz Republic to Alma Ata, Kazahkistan.

First person to bicycle 10,300 miles on entire Silk Web from Istanbul, Turkey to Xian, China.

Visited, studied, climbed, written, and lectured on scores of sacred mountains and ranges throughout the world including:

A. United States: Mt. Washington, N.H.; San Francisco and Sedona Peaks, Arizona; Tetons and Rocky Mountains in Idaho, Wyoming, and Colorado; Mt. Denali, Alaska; Cascades in California, Oregon, and Washington; Sierra Nevada in California; Peninsular Range in California and Mexico; Moana Loa, Moana Kai, Waimea in Hawaii

B. Sacred Mountains of California (Mt. Shasta, Kings Mountain, Squaw Peak, Mt. Diablo, Mt. Whitney, Junipero Serra, Mt. Pinos, Mt. Baldy, San Jacinto and Tarquiz, Mt. Cuchama, Mt. Davidson, and others.

C. Sacred Mountains of China: Heng Shan (North), Heng Shan (South), Omei Shan, Tai Shan, Hua Shan, and Sung Shan

D. Sacred Shugendo and Shinto Mountains of Japan, Fuji San, Omine Shan, Gassan and Yoduno Shan and Takachiho

E. Sacred Mountains of the Himalayas in India, Sikkim, Ladak, Kashmir, and Tibet Sacred Mountains of the World Journey: Mt. Lassen, California; Olympus, Greece; Mt. Athos, Aegean Sea; Mt. Tabor, Israel; Mt. Sinai, Sinai; Mt. Arunchala, India; Japanese Alps and Haleakala, Hawaii

F. Sacred Mountains and Places of Peru including Inca Trail, Machu Pichu, Isle of the Sun at Lake Titicaca, and Nasca Lines

G   Sacred Mountains of Africa: Kilimanjaro, Mt. Meru

Others: Mt. Subasio and Mt. Vesuvius, Italy; Swiss Alps and Ben Nevis, Scotland

Explorers Club Expedition Awards to "Advance the World's Knowledge" as to sacred mountains, the Silk Web history, travel, medicine (lipids and stamina), ethnology and spiritual architecture in Xingjiang, Tibet, Central Asia, Iran/Turkey, China, Mongolia, and Bhutan.

PUBLISHED BOOKS

To Climb a Sacred Mountain. A book about an around-the-world-in-40-days pilgrimage to climb Sacred Mountains to experience the religions of those mountains and understand the universal role of sacred mountains in personal spiritual experiences and in the metamorphosis of all religions (IWP Press 1976) The first book on this subject.

A Gift From The Master. Photography and Commentary in a book resulting from the author's journey with a modern day guru, Sri Darwin Gross

Water for California. A two volume legal reference book for water development, water rights, and water finance in California (with Harold Rogers; Bancroft-Whitney 1965)

Faces of China. A coffee table Book of Photography by Pat Fok with text by Alan Nichols as to the Sacred Mountains of China

San Quentin - Inside the Walls. Stories, history, and pictures of San Quentin Prison with photography and partial text by Alan Nichols (San Quentin Museum Association 1991)

San Francisco Commuter. Book of Poems written while commuting (Pendragon Press 1962)

Journey - A Bicycle Odyssey Through Central Asia. A story of a 3000 mile bicycle trip by the author and Keith Brown from Urumchi, Xingjiang on the western border of China, along the Silk Web, south across the Kun Lun and Karakoram Mountains and finally across Tibet to Lhassa via Kang Rimpoche [the world's most revered (in numbers at least) sacred mountain] (J.D. Huff 1991)

Adventures in Time. A book of poems written between 1952 and 2000 (Rygh Publishing 2000)

Travels with Annie. Short stories (Pendragon Press 2005)

Curriculum Guide for the Arts, Master Plan for Curriculum...San Francisco Public Schools

OTHER PUBLICATIONS

Annual Awards Publication, Ewald Foundation

Higher Ground: A Sacred Mountain Primer. San Francisco: J.D. Huff and Co, 1992.

Holy Chirripo...And The Can of Noodle Soup. Eldorado, Colo.: Sacred Mountain Press, 2005. *The*

Long Trek...Yosemite to Tahoe. San Francisco: Pendragon Press, 1944. (Contributor).

Adventurous Dreams, Adventurous Lives. Rocky Mountain Books, 2007.

(Contributor). *Quiet Beauty of China by Pat Pok.* Rizzoli International Publications, 1987.
San Quentin- Inside the Walls. San Quentin Museum Press, 1991.

Making Dreams Come True. Detroit Mich.: The Ewald Foundation, 1994. (Editor).

Our Children are Winners. Detroit Mich.: The Ewald Foundation, 1993. (Editor).

Welcome to the United Nations, Detroit Mich.: The Ewald Foundation, 1995. (Editor).
Who Am I? Detroit Mich.: The Ewald Foundation, 1997.

(Contributor) "Centennial Photography Competition," Explorers Journal, Fall 2003.

"Comment: How Not to Contest Special Assessments, or, You Can't Beat City Hall,"
Stanford Law Review 17, No. 2 (January 1965): 247-256.

Plays Authored and Produced

Siddartha. 1977 Grove Play. The life of Buddha (Bob Minser, Director)

Executive Christmas. Christmas play produced by the Bohemian Club as the Christmas Jinx in
1980 and 1994.

Executive Guru. Experimental play produced at Silverado Camp (Summer 1996. Bruce Bolt,
Director)

Articles

"The Public Interest," The American Bar Journal

"You Can't Fight City Hall," Stanford Law Review

"Constitutional Law Problems of Water Fluoridation," University of Southern California Law
Review

"Constitutional Law and Rights," Stanford Law Review

"Mt. Subasio," Mt. Takachiho," "Machu Pichu," "Letters Home" and other articles
and poetry in "Library Notes" of the Bohemian Club

New York Explorers Club Articles on Silk Web Cycling and other expeditions (Bhutan, Journey I
(Tibet), Journey II (Central Asia), Journey III (Turkey/Iran), Journey IV (China)

"The Return of the Dove...Tibet's Last Chance." Tibetan World 2008

"The Risky Road to Freedom...in the footsteps of the Dalai Lama" Explorers Journal

"Dead Men Tell Tales... Cinggis Qa'an Explorers Club Journal (scheduled for Fall 2011)

Several other legal, cycling, adventure, and sacred mountain articles

Major Unpublished Monograms and Works

Peaks of Gold. Photography and text about the sacred mountains of California

A Seven Day Spiritual Diet. A distillation of universal esoteric mystical practices for seven days
to discover one's natural spiritual inclination.

Darwin. A two volume biography of an American spiritual leader of a once powerful sect in California and worldwide.

A Gift to the Master. Photography and Commentary of a journey with a religious leader in Australia and South Asia.

Ishi. A play about America's last "wild" American Indian written as a Bohemian Grove Play. <u>The Messenger</u>. A play about the life of Mohammed.

The Toilet Papers. A book of poetry from the authors' experience as an undercover agent in San Francisco's prison (partially published in the San Francisco Examiner)

Hello Dalai. A story of an audience in 1972 with the Dalai Lama in Dharmsala, India

Letters Home. A play about a Stanford student who joins the French Army before the United States enters World War II, becomes a fighter pilot, and is shot down.

The Art of Loving...or Making it with Microna. A book of Sufi type poetry on love--human, technological, and spiritual

The Night Life of a School Board Member. A play about a single school board meeting about alleged pornography in school books.

Lama Krespi...Lessons from Yosemite to Tahoe. Lhamas on the Pacific Creek Trail. Movie script "The Return of the Dove." A story of the Dalai Lama's return to Tibet. The Rise and Fall of Tibet...The Dalai Lama, Inc.
Sacred Mountains of China. A description with pictures of the Five Sacred Mountains of China plus Omei Shan.

Mt. Kailas. A manuscript about Kang Rimpoche, in several respects the most important sacred mountain on the planet in Southwestern Tibet.

Honey Lake Reader. Short stories from the cattle country on the eastern slopes of the Sierras.
The Laughing Buddha. Short stories from Tibet and especially Mt. Kailas.

Others too many to mention.

EDUCATIONAL EXPERIENCES

Member, San Francisco Board of Education (President 1970-71)
Authored and coordinated Master Plan and Guidelines for Schools in San Francisco
Member, Board of Trustees, San Francisco City College (President 1971-72) Member,
Board of Trustees, Cathedral School for Boys (5 terms)
Board of Trustees, California College of Podiatric Medicine (associated with University of California San Francisco) San Francisco, California
Member, Board of Trustees, Prescott College, Sedona, Arizona
Member, Board of Governors, Webb Schools of California and Vivian Webb School, Claremont, California
Member of Special Finance Committee of California State Board of Education United States Army Instructor
University of California Extension, Real Estate Lecturer
Adjunct Professor of Forensic Medicine, California
College of Podiatric Medicine
Tibetologist

CIVIC EXPERIENCES

Member, San Francisco Library Commission
Director, Officer, San Francisco Junior Chamber of Commerce Member, Advisory Committee to Committee on Deferred Cost of
Education, sponsored by the U.S. Department of Health, Education and Welfare Member and President, Associates of Stanford University Libraries
Member and Chairman, William Saroyan Organizing Board and Advisory Board of Stanford University and the Saroyan Foundation
Member, San Francisco Special Civil Grand Jury to investigate City government
Active in the past with many community organizations and activities for which he was given the Distinguished Service Award (selected by the three San Francisco newspapers as the "Young Man of the Year")

LAW

President, The Nichols Professional Law Corporation (Attorneys at Law), specializing in municipal bonds and corporate finance, non-profit institutions, business and international banking

Former President, Nichols, Doi and Rappaport, Nichols and Rogers and Nichols, Rogers, Shreiner and Sperry

Arbitrator, American Arbitration Association

Admitted to practice before United States Supreme Court

Admitted to practice before all California Courts

Admitted to practice before several Districts of United States Federal Courts
Member, San Francisco, California, and American Bar Associations

A Rated attorney in Martindale Hubbel Bar Register of Preeminent Lawyers

LECTURER & PRODUCTIONS

Special Presentations

Dr. Buddy Rose; on the psychology of roses;

Press Conference with Ishi as last wild "Indian" in America

Lecturer on law, Sacred Mountains, travel, cycling the Silk Web, politics, Tibet, China, Bhutan, Sikim, Nepal, Central Asia (Turkmenistan, Uzbekistan, Tajikistan, Kyrgyzstan, Kazakhstan), Iran, Turkey, Mongolia

Expedition photographs and movies.

Photography: Photographer for Lectures, books (see below), articles, and presentations. Finalist, Centennial Photo Contest of the Explorers Club of New York and exhibition for 25 years at San Francisco's Bohemian Grove Art Gallery, several individual photography exhibits

BIOGRAPHICAL LISTINGS

Who's Who in the World Who's Who in the America
Who's Who in the California Who's Who in the West
Who's Who in the American Law
International Who's Who in Community Service Two Thousand Men of Achievement, 1972
Dictionary of International Biography
The Directory of Distinguished Americans
Notable Americans, American Biographical Institute Men of Achievement
Bar Register of Preeminent Lawyers, Martindale-Hubbell

ORGANIZATIONS

Several terms as member of Board of Directors, Burke's Tennis Club
Bohemian Club
San Francisco Stock Exchange Club
Faculty Club, Stanford University
Fellow, Vice Chair and Chair (San Francisco/Northern Califoprnia/Hawaii) Explorers Club
Ombudsman, and President, the Worldwide Explorers Club headquartered in New York City
Fellow, Royal Geographic Society, London
Alpine Club member
Delegate, United Nations NGO Committee.

FLAG EXPEDITIONS

XINGGIANG / TIBET MOUNTAIN BIKE EXPEDITION ...
... *May–July 1986*

CENTRAL ASIA BIKE EXPEDITION ...
Turkmenistan / Uzbekistan / Tajikistan / Turkestan / Kazahkstan ... *June – July 1993*

GANGKHAR PUENSUM ...
Bhutan's Sacred Mountain ... *September 2001*

CYCLING THE SILK WEB ...
Iran / Turkey ... *April 25 - June 2, 2004*

CYCLING THE SILK WEB ...
China / Kashgar / Xinggiang ... *April 10 – May 25, 2005*

PILGRIMAGE TO MONGOLIA ...
Sacred Mountains, Chinggis Qa'an, Roy Chapman Andrews ... *May 22 - July 1, 2010*

THE SEARCH FOR THE SECRET TOMB OF CHINGGIS QA'AN ...
Mongolia ... *September 2012*

SURVIVAL IN DEATH ...
Prairie Flora ... *July 26 - August 2, 2013*

Bibliography

Achenbach, Joel. "The Era of His Ways: In Which We Choose the Most Important Man of the Last Thousand Years." *The Washington Post,* 31 Dec., 1995.

Allsen, Thomas T. *Mongol Imperialism: The Policies of the Grand Qan Mongke in China, Russia, and the Islamic Lands.* Berkeley: University of California Press. 1987.

Culture and Conquest in Mongol Eurasia. Cambridge; New York: Cambridge University Press, 2002.

"The Circulation of Military Technology in the Mongolian Empire." In *Warfare in Inner Asian History,* 500–1800, ed. Nicola Di Cosmo, vol. 6 of *Handbook of Oriental Studies,* section 8: *Central Asia.* Leiden: Brill, 2002.

Atwood, Christopher Prat, *Encyclopedia of Mongolia and the Mongol Empire.* New York: Facts on File Library of World History, 2004.

Ayalon, David. "The Great Yasa of Chingiz Khan: A Reexamination." *Studia Islamica.* 1971-1973.

Black Belief, or Shamanism among the Mongols and Other Articles. Trans. Jan Nattier, and John R. Kreuger. *Mongolian Studies,* Journal of the Mongolia Society. 1991-1992.

Bazaarsad, N., B. Frohlich, N. Batbold, and D. Hunt. "Fourteenth Century Mummified Human Remains from the Gobi Desert, Mongolia." In *The Deer Stone Project: Anthropological Studies in Mongolia* 2002–2004, eds. William W. Fitzhugh, Jamsranjav Bayarsaikhan, and Peter K. Marsh. Washington, DC: Arctic Studies Center, National Museum of Natural History, Smithsonian Institution; Ulaan Bataar: National Museum of Mongolian History. 2001.

Bemmann, Jan, Hermann Parzinger, Ernst Pohl, and Damdinsuren Tseveendorj, eds. *Current Archaeological Research in Mongolia. Papers from the First International Conference on "Archaeological Research in Mongolia" held in Ulaanbaatar, August* 2007. Bonn Contributions to Asian Archaeology. 2009.

Berger, Patricia Ann, and Terese Tse Bartholomew. *Mongolia: The Legacy of Chinggis Khan.* London: Thames and Hudson in association with the Asian Art Museum of San Francisco. 2001.

Boyle, John A. *Successors of Genghis Khan.* New York: Columbia University Press. 1971.

Brose, Michael C. "Uyghur Technologists of Writing and Literacy in Mongol China." T' oung Pao 2005.

Subjects and Masters: Uyghurs in the Mongol Empire. Bellingham, WA: Center for East Asian Studies, Western Washington University. 2007.

Buell, Paul D. *Historical Dictionary of the Mongol World Empire.* No. 8 of *Historical Dictionaries of Ancient Civilizations and Historical Eras.* Lanham, MD: The Scarecrow Press. 2003.

Buyandelger, Manduhai. "Who Makes the Shaman?: The Politics of Shamanic Practices among the Buriats of Mongolia." *Inner Asia* I. 1999.

Caldwell, Taylor. *The Earth Is the Lord's: A Tale of the Rise of Genghis Khan.* New York: Amereon Ltd. 2001.

Chambers, James. *The Devil's Horsemen: The Mongol Invasion of Europe.* London: Atheneum. 1979.

Chaucer, Geoffrey. "The Squire's Tale." In *The Canterbury Tales,* trans. Ronald L. Ecker and Eugene J. Cook. Palatka, FL: Hodge & Braddock. 1993.

Crossley, Pamela Kyle. Making Mongols." In *Empire at the Margins: Culture, Ethnicity, and Frontier in Early Modern China,* ed. Pamela Kyle Crossley, Helen F. Siu, and Donald S. Sutton. Berkeley: University of California Press. 2006.

Crubezy, E., F. Ricaut, H. Martin, D. Erdenebaatar, H. Coqueugnot, B. Maureille, and P. Giscard. "Inhumation and Cremation in Medieval Mongolia: Analysis and Analogy." *Antiquity.* 2006.

Curtin, Jeremiah. *The Mongols: A History.* Boston: Little, Brown and Company. 1908.

Davi, Nicole K., Gordon C. Jacoby, Ashley E. Curtis, and Nachin Baatarbilcg. "Extension of Drought Records for Central Asia Using Tree Rings: West Central Mongolia." *Journal of Climate.* 2006.

De Rachewiltz, Igor, trans. *Yuan chao bi shih, The Secret History of the Mongols: A Mongolian Epic Chronicle of the Thirteenth Century.* Historical and philological commentary by Igor de Rachewiltz. 2 vols. *Brill's Inner Asian Library,* vol. 7. Leiden: Brill. 2004.

ed. *Military Culture in Imperial China.* Cambridge, MA: Harvard University Press. 2009.

Dion, Frederic. *The Blue Wolf: The Epic Tale of the Life of Genghis Khan and the Empire of the Steppes.* New York: Thomas Dunne Books. 2003.

Edwards, Mike. "Genghis: Lord of the Mongols." *National Geographic* 190. 1996.

Elverskog, Johan. "The Legend of Mount Muna." *Inner Asia* 8.

Fitzhugh, WIlliam W., Morris Rossabi, William Honeychurck, eds. *Genghis Khan and the Mongol Empire.* Sino Don Inc., The Mongolian Preservation Foundation *and* Arctic Studies Center, Smithsonian Institution. 2009.

Gernet, Jacques. Daily Life in China on the Eve of the Mongol Invasion, 1250–1276. Trans. H. M. Wright. New York: Macmillan. 1962.

Humphrey, Caroline. "Shamanic Practices and the State in Northern Asia: Views from the Center and Periphery." In *Shamanism, History and the State,* ed. N. Thomas and C. Humphrey. Ann Arbor: University of Michigan Press. 1994.

Shamans and Elders: Experience, Knowledge and Power among the Daur Mongo ls. Oxford: Oxford University Press. 1996.

Iggulden, Conn. *Genghis: Birth of an Empire.* New York: Delacorte Press. 2007.

Lords of the Bow. Bantam. 2010.

Bones of the Hills. Bantam. 2010.

Jenkins, Gareth. "A Note on Climate Cycles and the Rise of Chinggis Khan." *Central Asiatic Journal* 18. 1974.

Jobling, Mark A., and Chris Tyler-Smith. "The Human Y Chromosome: An Evolutionary Marker Comes of Age." *Nature Reviews Genetics* 4. 2003.

Juvaini [Juvaynî], 'Ata-Malik. *History of the World Conqueror.* Translated by John A. Boyle. 2 vols. Manchester: Manchester University Press. 1958.

Lamb, Harold. *Genghis Khan: The Emperor of All Men.* Garden City, NY: International Collectors Library. 1927.

Lattimore, Owen. "The Shrine of a Conqueror," *The Times* (London), 13 Apr. 1936.

Man, John. *Genghis Khan: Life, Death and Resurrection.* London: Bantam Press. 2005.

Martin, Henry Desmond. *The Rise of Chingis Khan and His Conquest of North China.* Baltimore: Johns Hopkins University Press. 1970.

May, Timothy. *The Mongol Art of War.* London: Pen and Sword Publications. 2007.

Miyake, Toshihiko. "Coins Collected from the Avraga Site." In *Avraga* I: *Occasional Paper on the Excavations of the Palace of Genghis Khan,* ed. Shimpei Kato and Noriyuki Shiraishi. Tokyo: Doseisha. 2005.

Nam, Seng Geung. "A Study of Military Technics [sic] of the Thirteenth Century Mongols." Mongolica. 1994.

Nichols, Alan Hammond. *To Climb a Sacred Mountain.* Illuminated Way Press. *1979*

Journey: A Bicycle Odyssey Through Central Asia. J. D. Huff and Company. 1991.

Pohl, Ernst. "Interpretation without excavation: Topographical mapping on the ground of the Mongolian capital Karakorum." In *Current Archaeological Research in Mongolia. Papers from the First International Conference on "Archaeological Research in Mongolia" held in Ulaanbaatar, August 2007,* ed. Jan Bemmann Hermann Parzinger, Ernst Pohl, Damdinsuren Tseveendorj. Bonn: Bonn University. 2009.

Polo, Marco. *The Travels of Marco Polo*: The Complete Yule-Cordier Edition.

Prawdin, Michael. *The Mongol Empire: Its Rise & Legacy.* Routledge. 2005.

151

Sinor, Denis. "On Mongol Strategy." In *Proceedings of the Fourth East Asian Altaistic Conference,* ed. Ch'en Chieh-hsien. Tainan, Taiwan: Dept. of History, National Ch'engkung University. 1971.

Smith, John Masson, Jr. "Mongol and Nomadic Taxation." *Harvard Journal of Asiatic Studies* 30. 1970.

"Mongol Society and Military in the Middle East: Antecedents and Adaptations." In *War and Society in the Eastern Mediterranean, 7th and 15th Centuries,* vol. 9. of *The Medieval Mediterranean Peoples, Economies, and Cultures,* 400-1453, ed. Yaacov Lev. Leiden: Brill. 1996.

Spuler, Bertold. *History of the Mongols.* Reprint of 1972 *History of the Mongols, Based on Eastern and Western Accounts of the Thirteenth and Fourteenth Centuries.* Trans. from the German by Helga and Stuart Drummond. Berkeley: University of California Press; New York: Dorset Press. 1989.

Toynbee, Arnold Joseph. *A Study of History.* 12 vols. London; New York: Oxford University Press. 1934-1961.

Vladimirtsov, Boris Iakovlevich. *The Life of Chingis Khan.* Trans. by D.S. Mirsky. Reprint of 1930 ed. New York: Benjamin Blom. 1969.

Wade, Nicholas. "A Prolific Genghis Khan, It Seems, Helped People the World," *New York Times,* 11 Feb. 2003.

Weatherford, Jack [McIver]. *Genghis Khan and the Making of the Modern World.* New York: Crown Publishers.

The Secret History of the Mongol Queens. 2004.

YCC (The Y Chromosome Consortium) "A Nomenclature System for the Tree of Human Y-Chromosome Binary Haplogroups." Genome Research. 2002.

Zerjal, Tatiana, et. Al. "The Genetic Legacy of the Mongols." American Journal of Human Genetics. 2003.

Zhi-Yong Yin, Xuemei Shao, Ningsheng Qin, and Eryuan Liang. "Reconstruction of a 1436-year Soil Moisture and Vegetation Water Use History Based on Tree-ring Widths from Qilian Junipers in Northeastern Qaidam Basin, Northwestern China." *International journal of Climatology.* 2007.

Index

CPSIA information can be obtained
at www.ICGtesting.com
Printed in the USA
BVHW020320060222
628027BV00002B/7